THE COVETed
LEADER

5 Pillars of Transformative Leadership

Fazl Siddiqui

The COVETed Leader:
5 Pillars of Transformative Leadership

Copyright © Fazl Siddiqui, 2017
All rights reserved.

ISBN 13: 978-1-944027-37-7 (paperback)
ISBN 13: 978-1-944027-36-0 (ebook)

Cupiditas Publishing

CONTENTS

Dedication 5

Introduction 7

1. The Journey Begins 17

2. What is a Leader? 21

3. Courage 27

4. Optimism 51

5. The Office Visit 79

6. Vision 91

7. Excellence 121

8. Trust 143

9. A Final Word 173

Acknowledgements 175

DEDICATION

To the true COVETed leaders in my life – my mother who was responsible for bringing me in this world, she was wise like a hermit; compassionate as a saint; pure as nectar; strong like a mountain…she was a fighter, she was courageous, she loved life and her spirits were always high and soared like an eagle, she reached out to all and sundry like an ocean – she was magnanimous, she was benevolent, she was gentle, she was kind, she was patient, she was persistent, she had integrity and she had character!

My father who was powerful like dynamite and a true perfectionist and a disciplinarian who instilled in me values that helped me be the person I am today. He was an extremely ambitious and hardworking man who taught me the value of unconditional dedication to your work. He was an incredibly pious soul who lived life fully yet when he left he left like a new born baby.

My father-in-law a great person who always had an aura of security and a rare-air sense of stability about him that one always felt safe and secure around him. He was such a magnanimous and towering personality that we felt dwarfed but not belittled or small. He was a giver all his life, but he used wisdom and exercised prudence to decide who would be the receiver and how much, he was a 'conditional giver', someone who could not be taken for a ride, or be moved by feign sob-stories. He was an incredibly contented person who was so comfortable living with bare minimum yet being extremely generous in fulfilling the requests of those in genuine need.

May they all rest in peace!

INTRODUCTION

Ralph Waldo Emerson wrote a poem called "The Mountain and the Squirrel." In it, the mountain calls the squirrel "Little Prig" and says that because he – the mountain carries the forest on his shoulders and, therefore, he is very important.

The little squirrel responds that although she is tiny and could not carry a forest on her back, the mountain could not crack a nut. Basically, she is pointing out that each of us has our unique talents. This is the beauty and power behind the concept of the COVETed Leader.

I started my journey and exploration to understand my unique talents more than fifteen years ago. I now am honored to share my insights from my journey with you, which will hopefully help you take your own insightful journey and explore how to become a COVETed Leader.

I begin with an overview of the paths leadership has taken, often missing the rich, wondrous, everyday path of the COVETed Leader. It's about not making leadership a scary journey. Rather, becoming a leader is an *everyday journey*, one that is accessible to each one of us. Yes, that means you, too.

So consider the phrase **Let Every Act of yours Define you**. Here the phrase reveals the *you* through the wisdom of the COVETed Leader. But let me first provide a brief overview of the history of leadership to help you see the clearer road to a different and more accessible leadership path for you.

The Leadership Pathway

Traditionally, people were believed to have been "born to be a leader." Leadership skills were something you had or you didn't have. If you were a leader, you were genetically lucky, and if you weren't, nothing you did could change who you were. Known as "The Great Man Theory," leadership was a trait like height, eye color, or athletic ability. If you were a born leader, your abilities made you part of a divine class. People believed that leaders and followers were almost different species.

Supporters of this leadership-exclusivity viewpoint argued that every society singled out intellectually and morally superior individuals. It was believed that they were the divinely appointed leaders of every society. Fortunately, the leadership DNA myth has been debunked, and Plato's "elitist phenomena" has been disproven.

In our study of leadership over the decades, we have learned that true leaders all have a burning desire to lead, to be influential and motivational, to take responsibility for themselves and others, and to stand out and to be sought after. They don't have a *natural* ability for leadership, but they do have a great desire to lead people. That desire, coupled with a drive to succeed and standout, combined with a set of learned skills that they apply as leaders, is what makes them leaders.

Even so, some of these leaders are better than others. They have become the best by practicing and learning from their leadership practice. Nearly all of them can remember specific times when they were either called up to lead, forced to assume leadership, or had a leadership role assigned to them. Nearly all of them would say the starting point for their leadership journey began at the intersection of a desire to lead and learning *how* to lead.

The only real qualifying element they possessed when they began leading was an unquenchable drive to lead and excel at it. They had to learn the rest of it. The skills and traits that they learned from a variety of mentors, situations, and experiences—both successful and unsuccessful—were what put them ahead of others and made others look up to them so they became COVETed© leaders.

The State of Leadership in America

Study after study shows our current leaders are failing us. Two Gallup Polls are among the most damning reports. First, in a 2013 "State of the American

Workplace" report, Gallup interviewed nearly 150,000 workers–people from all states and in all industries. They discovered that a stunning number—70%—are miserable in their jobs. More specifically, only 30% of the nation's working population admitted to being fully engaged at work.[1]

Compared to the 13% of happy-and-fully-engaged workers worldwide,[2] the USA is doing better than most, but not by much. Gallup researchers also interviewed workers in 142 countries, including the U.S., and found that 87% of the world's working class are miserable.[3] So what's causing seven out of every 10 workers to be so miserable that they disengage and under-commit themselves at work?

Lack of Leadership

When leadership experts say many people go through their whole lives having no real sense of their talents or if they have a passion or purpose in life, they are definitely onto something real and provable. Valuable human resources are like any desirable natural resource. They're often buried deep and take time and expense to extract. But given the right meaning and environment, it is possible to tap latent human potential through nurture and care, resulting in a workforce that is indeed engaged, committed, and valuable.

Unfortunately, most organizations spend so much time celebrating the people who *claim* to be leaders and they overlook the true leaders.[4] Human resource departments typically thrust the most politically astute, aggressive, or assertive employee into a leadership position simply because "the squeaky wheel gets the grease." These people generally have no leadership skills or experience at all. They simply know how to advance their own careers. HR departments, managers, and supervisors do this because they don't have a better candidate or

---

1 https://www.fastcompany.com/3011032/gallups-workplace-jedi-on-how-to-fix-our-employee-engagement-problem
2 http://news.gallup.com/poll/165269/worldwide-employees-engaged-work.aspx
3 http://news.gallup.com/poll/165269/worldwide-employees-engaged-work.aspx
4 http://municipalinnovators.ca/mic-conferences/2016-conference/2016-agenda

they don't understand what makes a true leader. Even the most senior members of a company have convinced themselves that these are the only people worth following and looking up to, to provide leadership.

As a result of those choices, we start to devalue the incredible things that ordinary people around us do. Instead, we become believers in self-proclaimed or self-appointed leaders. Therefore, moments where we or others exhibit leadership become insignificant. In fact, we end up not taking credit for some of the extraordinarily fulfilling acts that we make as ordinary people. We also then don't let ourselves feel good about our ordinary, yet important, acts of leadership. The true leaders languish, unrecognized because people don't understand what it truly means to be a leader.

It's not surprising that *confidence* in business leaders is at a record low.[5] Following are a few statistical surveys and analyses of data from the corporate world.

An opinion poll by Edelman in 2014 showed that fewer than 50% of respondents trusted chief executives.[6]

Another recent poll for *Parade* magazine found that 35% of American employees would forgo a substantial pay raise if they could see their direct supervisors fired.[7]

A recent review of academic literature concluded that "one in every two leaders and managers" is judged "ineffective (that is, a disappointment, incompetent, or a complete failure) in their current roles."[8]

Even bosses are turning on their fellow bosses. In 2011, nearly a sixth of the world's 2,500 biggest firms fired their CEOs.[9]

---

5 https://www.hrgrapevine.com/content/article/2009-08-04-us-ceo-confidence-falls-to-record-low
6 https://www.economist.com/news/business-books-quarterly/ 21672016-pay-attention-mundane-things-business-life-getting-it-right
7 https://www.forbes.com/sites/meghancasserly/2012/10/17/majority-of-americans-would-rather-fire-their-boss-than-get-a-raise/
8 https://www.economist.com/news/business-books-quarterly/21672016-pay-attention-mundane-things-business-life-getting-it-right
9 https://www.economist.com/news/business-books-quarterly/ 21672016-pay-attention-mundane-things-business-life-getting-it-right

The question is *what can be done to improve this lamentable state of affairs?* Three books (there are hundreds) from recognized experts provided different answers.

In 2003, Bill George, a former CEO of Medtronic who teaches at Harvard Business School (HBS) and the author of *Discover Your True North,* and some of his colleagues challenged older models of leadership, including the "Great Man Theory" and competency-based leadership models. They claimed that business people spent more time trying to "market" themselves as leaders, rather than undertaking the transformative work that leadership development requires. These insights led to their book, *Authentic Leadership.* They proposed a new kind of leader, with character as the ingredient that mattered most.[10] They claimed that leaders must become more authentic to earn their followers' trust, and they outlined the following qualities as essential part of a leader's character:

According to George, authentic leaders demonstrate five qualities. They are:

- Understanding their purpose
- Practicing solid values
- Leading with heart
- Establishing connected relationships
- Demonstrating self-discipline[11]

The Harvard Business Review supported this view and in 2015 declared, "Authenticity has emerged as the gold standard for leadership."[12] The debate over which form of leadership works best seemed almost settled, and many leading international companies started focusing on developing "authentic

---

10 http://www.lifeworkleadership.org/Authentic-Leadership
11 http://www.lifeworkleadership.org/Authentic-Leadership
12 https://hbr.org/2015/01/the-authenticity-paradox

leaders" within their ranks. Executive courses on authentic leadership development at Harvard Business School are oversubscribed and expanding every year.[13]

Jim Kouzes and Barry Posner have completed comprehensive work on leadership and continue to study the topic. They suggest that leadership is not about personality. It's about behavior—an observable set of skills and abilities—and about what great leaders actually do when they are at their personal best.[14]

They developed "The Five Practices of Exemplary Leadership® Model". They identified these practices as:

- Being an exemplary role model
- Having an inspiring vision
- Challenging assumptions and removing roadblocks
- Enabling talent
- Celebrating success[15]

In 2015, Jeffrey Pfeffer—who hails from Harvard Business School's great rival on the West Coast, the Stanford Graduate School of Business—took a completely different approach in his much acclaimed and hugely controversial book *Leadership BS*. His book maintained that what the leadership industry needs is "less warm waffle and more hard-headed realism, arguing that 'the last thing a leader needs to be at crucial moments is authentic.'"

And Wharton's Adam Grant wrote in the New York Times, "'Be yourself' is actually a terrible advice … Nobody wants to see your true self."[16]

Another professor from INSEAD, Herminia Ibarra, argued, "We have to find a way to fake it till we become it."[17]

---

13 http://hbswk.hbs.edu/item/the-truth-about-authentic-leaders
14 http://www.leadershipchallenge.com/about-section-our-approach.aspx
15 http://www.leadershipchallenge.com/about.aspx
16 https://www.nytimes.com/2016/06/05/opinion/sunday/unless-youre-oprah-be-yourself-is-terrible-advice.html?_r=0
17 https://en.wikipedia.org/wiki/Fake_it_till_you_make_it

Further, with the emergence of such contradicting theories, leadership has become an even more perplexing and dramatic subject, something huge, something bigger than us, something beyond us, something scary. Leadership has been made into a challenge, a larger-than-us purpose, changing the world. And the title of leader has long been treated as if it's something that one day we're going to deserve, something we're going to become worthy of. Despite all this debate and theories being developed and flaunted all over, the sad part is that:

- Leadership has not improved. In fact, the quality of leaders has rapidly deteriorated.
- Most people disagree with or do not think highly of their leaders.
- Trust in leaders is at an abysmal low.
- Leaders who defy every rule in the book shockingly become successful.
- Egotistic leaders land in leadership positions, perchance by either being born to a certain family or getting lucky by being in the right place at the right time.

There are yet no universally accepted courses or interventions that guarantee development of future leaders.

I then stumbled upon the work of Drew Dudley, who believes that we routinely ignore a huge percentage of the leadership that exists around us in our day-to-day lives, and this can perhaps be remedied by helping individuals and organizations create "cultures of everyday leadership" through daily acts of leadership.[18]

In his wildly popular TED talk,[19] Dudley called these everyday acts "Lollipop Moments"—a concept that has resonated well with me and thousands of people around the world.

It is ironic that despite witnessing acts of leadership as commonplace and everyday by ordinary people, we seldom give that title to ourselves and somehow

---

18 https://xtracredits.com/faculty/drew-dudley/
19 https://www.ted.com/talks/drew_dudley_everyday_leadership

consider our acts as demonstrations of arrogance. So redefining leadership, I thought, was probably the most befitting mission today.

Most of us *undervalue* everyday acts of genuine leadership and *overvalue* positional leadership, even when a formally appointed leader, one who has accidentally inherited it, does an extremely pathetic job and is driven by arrogance, pride, and power.

Everything you will ever do as a leader is based on the one simple, yet audacious assumption—that you matter. Before you can lead others, you have to lead yourself. You have to believe that you can have a positive impact on others. You have to believe that your words can inspire and your actions can move others. You have to believe that what you do counts. If you don't, you won't even try. Leadership begins with YOU!

LEAD : Let **E**very **A**ct of yours **D**efine you!

As I introduced earlier, the concept of LEAD can help you find, nurture, and develop your inborn leadership talents. If we can learn to lead ourselves, we can lead others, and in the short time we're here in this world, we will be able to make a difference in the world. You don't have to be a Bill Gates or a Mother Theresa to make a profound difference.

Oscar Wilde once said, "Be yourself. Everyone else is already taken".

The quest for leadership, therefore, is first an inner quest to discover who you are and what you care about, and, second, it's through a process of self-examination that you will develop the awareness necessary to lead. Self-confidence is about awareness of and faith in your own powers. Additionally, these powers grow as you work to identify and develop them. The mastery of the art of leadership comes with the mastery of the self, and so developing leadership is a process of developing the self, yet remaining humble.[20]

"To become a leader, then, you must become yourself; become the maker of your own life." Leadership expert, Warren Bennis, observes that knowing yourself is "the most difficult task any one of us faces. But until you truly know

---

[20] http://www.leadertoleaderjournal.com/article-print-page/leadership-inner-journey.aspx

yourself, your strengths and weaknesses, know what you want to do and why you want to do it, you cannot succeed."[21]

Living a life of authenticity generates openness where relationships are impacted where all involved benefit. Here, the path is about being true to yourself, congruent, bold, and authentic. These strong results manifest because when you really believe and accept who you are, you create that unique space where you have been born to live and thrive.

You must genuinely believe that you are never more beautiful than when you're ugly, you're never stronger than when you are vulnerable, you are never more enough than when you are scared, you're never more perfect than when you are imperfect—because that's when you really know who you are and what you're made of.

In leadership, being genuine implies that we are embodying our true selves into our leadership role. Being true to yourself calls you to draw on the very essence of your values, beliefs, principles, and morals that become your *guiding compass.*[22]

Marianne Williamson once said, "Our greatest fear is not that we are inadequate. Our greatest fear is that we are powerful beyond measure. It is our light, and not our darkness, that frightens us."

Being truthful, or saying your truth, demands self-accountability to realize the mistakes and correct them. The more you become truthful, the more you become beneficial to your family, friends, and the society, and you even help make their lives meaningful and fulfilling.[23]

This led to the development of the concept of "The COVETed Leader." The word 'covet' comes from the Latin word *cupiditas*, meaning "passionate desire, eagerness, ambition."

Coveted is another way of saying "sought after."

---

[21] Book: Contemporary Issues in Leadership by By William E. Rosenbach, Robert L. Taylor, Mark A. Youndt
[22] https://www.insights.com/us/resources/authentic-leadership/
[23] http://nypspb.blogspot.com/2016/02/

Ella Wheeler Wilcox said, "If you are seeking usefulness, skill in any direction, there is nothing and no one who can hinder your attainment of the coveted boon, if you are willing to work and wait."[24]

So when you think about your identity. When you think about what it means to be alive. Further, when you think about why you deserve to exist in this world and why you are 'your unique self' among the seven and half billion people in this world, you need to find that leader in you who makes a positive impact on others' lives. You also make others feel bigger and better than who they are!

Come with Me on a Wondrous Journey

Now that you have been introduced to the COVETed Leader in you, join me to explore what your new life can look like. For it is in the journey, not the destination that true ownership of the Coveted Leader in you will come alive and thrive.

---

24 http://www.finestquotes.com/author_quotes-author-Ella%20Wheeler%20Wilcox-page-0.htm

Chapter One

THE JOURNEY BEGINS

"I hate you! I never ever want to work for you," screamed 16-year-old Adam as he stormed out of the coffee shop. He and his father Alex had been having breakfast and discussing plans for his summer job. Alex, the CEO of a small midwestern manufacturing plant, shook his head before taking a sip of coffee and pulling out his cell phone. He had been just like his son when he had been 16, but he still didn't understand where Adam's anger came from.

"My kids told me the same thing," a smiling soft-spoken gentleman said as he approached the table. "Bad timing," he said. "But your table happens to have the only real sugar in the place." He gestured towards the packets of sweetener on the table.

"Oh, no problem," Alex said, pushing the container towards the man.

"Mike," the man said, extending his hand.

"Alex." The two men shook hands. He studied the man's face. He knew him from somewhere. Work or pleasure. He couldn't be sure, but probably work. That look in his eyes, and his calm confidence said executive—retired maybe, but definitely an executive.

"It gets better," Mike said.

"What does?"

"Teenage sons," Mike said, cocking his head to one side. "One of mine told me the same thing twenty years ago. Now he's the CEO of my company, and I couldn't pry him out of his office with dynamite."

"Really?" Alex said, putting down his cell phone. "How'd you manage that?" He had been right. Executive.

"If you really want to know, call me. Set up a time to talk, and I'll tell you." Mike dug in his pocket for a card and handed it to Alex.

"It's old, but the contact info is still good." He laughed, took his sugar, and turned to leave. Alex glanced at the card, then at Mike as he disappeared into the breakfast crowd. Mike Davis! Alex all but did a face plant as he kicked himself for not recognizing him. Davis had founded the largest manufacturing company in the world, and had then gone on to become a serial entrepreneur. He was worth billions. And he had invited Alex to meet with him. Why? He'd soon find out. Within two weeks, the men had scheduled breakfast at Mike's home office.

"Why me?" Alex asked after they exchanged greetings and shook hands.

"Hearing your son tell you the same thing mine told me." Mike shook his head. "Something about that whole scene made it feel like it was yesterday when my son told me the same thing. I guess I just wanted to help. Besides," he smiled, "I know who you are, and what your company does. We need you and your company to stick around and grow. Consider my meddling an investment in the industry as well."

Alex felt embarrassed and at a disadvantage, but he just smiled and said, "Thank you."

Mike led Alex out onto a huge patio overlooking a swimming pool and a luxurious garden. As they sat down at a table, two uniformed waiters served them breakfast.

"Now, tell me about your son," Mike said.

"Adam's a teenager. He likes sports, music, cars, and computers. Smart kid, but he has his mother's tendency to be over dramatic." Alex shrugged. "I want him to work with me full-time in the plant this summer and start learning the business. He wants to play."

"Play?" Mike asked.

"You know, goof off, hang with his friends, start wasting his life," Alex said.

The Journey Begins

Alex could feel his bitterness and anger creeping in. He had two sons, Adam, the smart one, and David, his sweet, but clumsy and non-business oriented 13-year-old. David would never want to run a business, but Adam? Adam was sharp. If he paid attention and worked at it, he'd easily be able to fill Alex's shoes when the time came. Except now, he didn't want to.

For the next two hours, the men discussed their sons. Then Alex said, "How do I make him want to work for me?"

"You don't."

"What?"

"You don't. You can't make anyone do something he/she doesn't want to do," Mike said. "The best you can do is make yourself the kind of leader people want to follow, and then hope that your son wants and chooses to follow you. Changing oneself is much harder than forcing other people to change, but it's also much more effective."

"What do I have to do?" Alex asked.

"That's exactly the question I was hoping for." He turned to wave at one of the waiters standing silently by the kitchen door. The man came over, bringing a pad of paper and a pen for Alex.

"Take notes," Mike said. "You're going to need them."

Chapter Two

WHAT IS A LEADER?

"Are you a leader? Or just the CEO?" Mike asked.

Alex laughed. "Is there a difference? You can't be one without the other," he said.

"Can't you?"

Alex stopped. He'd never thought about it.

"We assume people are leaders if they're CEOs, or executives, or in a position of power," Mike said. "They may be in charge, but they're not always leaders. On the other hand, there are many people who hold no official or formal position but are extremely great and gifted leaders.

"No matter what leadership definition or example you use, or believe in I think the one quality every leader, every person really, should have is authenticity," Mike said. He became very serious.

"I've watched you over the years, Alex. I think you are authentic, most of the time anyway. None of us are perfect, but you're the real deal. I trust my gut, my instincts."

"Authentic?" Alex asked. "I just don't have time for games or pretending to be something or someone I'm not."

Mike laughed. "The words of someone who is truly authentic!"

Alex cocked his head to one side, confused. "I'm curious. Exactly what do you mean by an authentic leader?"

"Well, let me tell you a story about someone I consider an authentic leader. A man by the name of Captain William Swenson was awarded the Congressional

Medal of Honor for his actions in Afghanistan on September 8, 2009. I only read the news account and saw the video. I wish I could have known what was going through his head. What struck me about him was that he acted on his feelings, without worrying about what anyone thought of him or his actions."

"I guess in war that's a must," Alex said.

"Maybe, but not like this. According to the story I read," Mike continued, "American and Afghan troops were protecting Afghan officials meeting with village elders. The group came under attack, and Swenson took charge, running into live fire to save his men and rescue the wounded. Someone was wearing a GoPro camera and recorded the whole thing. Swenson and another soldier were carrying a wounded man to a medevac helicopter. He was the first man rescued, and there were others needing immediate assistance, but before he left the injured man, Swenson bent down and kissed the man on the forehead—like a father might kiss his own son—before leaving to rescue other men. I don't know. All I could think of was my own son and whether I could have, would have done that. It was very moving to me.

"Where does love and connection like that come from? Under fire and he's still able to take time to reach out to his men. I'm sure he felt like this about all of them, and this wasn't the first time he let them know he cared. I asked myself, 'Do I work with people I care about this deeply? Do the people who work for me care about me at all?' It stopped me in my tracks."

"What was your answer?" Alex asked.

"No! It was an emphatic 'no,' too. And that was a shock. I thought, 'Was it that this was the military service where there's all this life and death stuff?' I spent a lot of time dissecting exactly what generated this kind of intense loyalty and caring. I believe it was the environment, not the work, not the military career over business. I thought that if I can create an environment that celebrates sacrifice, engagement, connection, and mutual trust among the people who create it, I can create this same environment in my plant. My employees will be moved and motivated to achieve remarkable things. I believed that I could create more with trust and respect than competition.

What is a Leader?

I've met a lot of heroes, from astronauts to military men and women, to police officers and firemen, as well as my employees. And I made it a point to read all I could about people recognized for a heroic act. When the reporter says, 'Why did you do it? Why did you risk your life for this person?' in almost every case, if they knew the person they say, 'I know they would have done it for me.' And if they didn't know the person they say, 'I think they would have done the same for me.' They have a sense of trust and belief in the people around them because they operate in the kind of environment that promotes that sort of feeling."

"Wow," Alex said. "I can't imagine risking my life for a stranger, or even an employee." He was silent for a moment. "You know, I can't even remember the last time I kissed my own son, let alone a stranger."

"It's not the kiss as much as it is the emotions and thoughts behind it," Mike said. "He was communicating a depth of feeling that words couldn't express.

"Let me tell you another case that moved me. I have a lot of friends in the Middle East. One of them once told me about a young leader who showed up so authentically that it shocked not just the employees and his bosses but the entire nation. This person worked in the oil sector. There was once a terrible accident at a hydrocracker unit of the refinery, and people died in the blast.

"I don't know if you know about the oil industry. They work in scary conditions. It's like sitting on a time bomb. Anyway, it took six years to rebuild the refinery. Although all safety conditions were met and extra care was taken to ensure the refinery met international safety standards, there was still an air of uncertainty and caution; and nobody wanted to be the first to operate the hydrocracker unit, and workers were very reluctant to enter the unit.

"My friend tells me about this young leader who is still pretty inexperienced but decided to demonstrate authentic leadership skills and went down into the unit first. It was long after he had gone in with a team of workers and operated the unit along with them that his management got to know of this incident, and they all rushed to the refinery from the head office. But all they could do was to stay outside to greet him when he returned after getting the unit operational. When asked why he did that, his response was, "For each of us, our life is precious, and if I can ask any of my workers to risk his life, I should be willing to risk mine, too."

"How is that authentic?" Alex said.

"Well, contrary to popular belief, authenticity isn't about expressing your genuine self in every situation. It's more about knowing yourself so well you know which part of you to show to the world at the appropriate time," Mike replied.

"I don't get it," Alex said.

"Authenticity isn't about revealing everything you're thinking, feeling, wanting, or chasing after. It's about unbiased self-examination and a deep knowledge of self. You act from a place of personal responsibility, humility, and empathy. You know yourself so well you're willing to listen to feedback from others because you can recognize the truth in it. You can see their projection as well as your own. You can say your truth, but more importantly, you can genuinely seek the truth in others.

"Authenticity is complicated. We all tell ourselves so many stories, and we trust all of our illusions and biases. We deceive ourselves, engage in wishful thinking, and have a tendency to behave differently when we know others are watching. I read somewhere that we suffer from what the writer described as "ADD - Authenticity Deficit Disorder." As difficult as it is to be authentic, the closer we get to it, the better leaders we become.

"Your homework this week is to learn all you can about authenticity. Authenticity is the foundation for the COVETed leadership style."

"Coveted?"

"Yes, Courage, Optimism, Vision, Excellence, Trust. To covet something means to desire it passionately, but more than that, to yearn or thirst for it. Coveted leadership isn't just your standard leadership model. It's more. It requires heart, passion, and love as well as certain skill sets. Anyone can be taught to manage or lead people. It takes a lot more to become a coveted leader, one people will follow through hell. COVETed leaders will always make a positive impact, also helping others around them feel bigger and better," Mike said.

What is a Leader?

Alex laughed nervously. "I don't know that I have what it takes to lead people through hell, or to make people feel bigger than they think they are" he said. "But I'm willing to find out."

"Good. That's all I ask. By the way, Coveted leaders are not necessarily gifted or born with special privileges. These are ordinary people with ordinary dreams who make theirs and the lives of those around them extraordinarily fulfilling. But remember, finding out what authenticity and leadership is, also means finding out what it is not. You have your homework, so get started."

* * *

Alex shifted his briefcase from one hand to the other as he waited for Mike to answer the door. He'd spent more time than he should have reading all he could about authenticity, and he still wasn't sure he understood what Mike was talking about. Adam had spent the night at a friend's house and still wasn't speaking to him. He wasn't sure how all this leadership talk was going to help him change that. He felt alone, inadequate, confused, and a bit angry. Was that authentic?

"Ah, Alex. Come on in." Mike opened the door, stepping back to wave Alex in. "Still confused, I see."

"How?"

"I was a CEO for a billion-dollar company for ten years," Mike laughed. "It's my job to know when people are confused or angry." He looked at Alex kindly. "I told you it wouldn't be *easy but believe me it'll definitely be worth it,*" he said.

"You did." Alex walked out to the poolside table and set his briefcase down before sitting heavily in the chair in the deepest shade.

Mike sat down beside him, reaching for a pitcher of tea and pouring them both a glass.

"Search the internet for leaders and leadership, and you'll find millions of articles, opinions, and books on leadership," Mike said. "But let me save you the research time. After years as a CEO, investor, and philanthropist, and the father of a teenaged boy, I've condensed the secrets of what it means to be a leader into what I call "The Five Pillars," the ones I told you about last week. They stand for: Courage, Optimism, Vision, Excellence and Trust. These pillars represent what I call the "COVETed" leader, meaning intense and passionate desire or sought after.

"What I want to do is meet with you once a month for the next six months and discuss each quality. You'll have homework in between each meeting, like you just did. I think if you do your homework, you'll see some pretty profound changes in your life, in your relationship with your son, and in your business."

"Thank you," Alex said. "I'm in. But what can I do for you?"

"You can be my guinea pig," Mike said. "I'm generous, but I'm not Santa Claus. I want an executive, someone of your caliber and business holdings to prove my concept of leadership in real time. Your son is not unlike many teenagers of family-owned corporations. I think we can save manufacturing and family businesses with my concept. And perhaps this is the most appropriate time to redefine leadership. Are you still in?"

"Even more, if that's possible," Alex said.

"Perfect. Then let's get started," Mike said. He leaned back in his chair. "And, let's start with Courage."

Chapter Three

COURAGE

"I'm going to go all professor on you here," Mike said. "What you're doing with Adam, with yourself, with me, it's all going to take courage. I don't mean the Hollywood superhero version of courage. I mean the kind of courage men don't talk about, but that we all recognize when we see it."

Alex nodded solemnly. He knew exactly what Mike was talking about.

"Courage is not, as many believe, an act of the fearless, or the warrior," Mike continued. "Courage is about acting on something even when you're afraid. It's that precise ability to hold both fear and bravery in our minds and hearts that makes courage such an admirable trait. We think it's uncommon, but it's not. It's a trait achievable by us all."

"How is that 'going all professor' on me?" Alex asked.

"That's not. This is," Mike said. He dug into his shirt pocket for his reading glasses as he pulled a page out of a folder in front of him. He began to read,

Courage is defined as *the ability to select between two rights and act on it with conviction, or to differentiate between two wrongs and say which is wrong and why, honestly.* This would be the case even if you are afraid—if you are in the company of your boss or your seniors and especially your peers. You're telling them, 'I'm saying my truth. I'm taking ownership. This strength comes from my deep-rooted core values.' This also relates to self compassion. You are acting on your thoughts and decisions with conviction. The whole world may say it is wrong, but you are taking ownership of your values. That is a direct quote from my human resources director.

Alex started to speak, but Mike held up his hand, signaling for silence.

"This is the professor." He began to read again.

"The word 'courage' derives from the Old French word *corage*, meaning 'heart or innermost feelings,' and from the Latin word *cor* for 'heart.' In Middle English, the word was used broadly to mean 'bravery' but linked to negative traits that may hinder it such as wrath, pride, confidence, lustiness, etc. Today, courage asks us to show absolute strength in silencing those demons, distractions, and downsides that derail us along the way. It requires us to live in discomfort while we pursue the passions that drive us in all aspects of our lives.

"Okay, remember Swenson? We often think of Courage with a capital C, like in a battle or a personal sacrifice only the best and bravest of us must face. But it isn't about that. Where courage truly makes an impact is in the relationships we create and develop with one another.

"You, my friend, are on the cusp of making or breaking a very important relationship with your son. Without courage, that first pillar of leadership, you're not going to go very far."

"I don't understand," Alex said. "Relationship? Adam and I are father and son. We're family. We have a relationship, even if it is in shambles right now. What do you mean courage?"

"Okay. Let me tell you about a woman named Elizabeth Lesser." Mike pushed a book towards Alex. "Read this later. It's her book. She writes about her sister Maggie's fight against an aggressive form of cancer. Maggie had to have a bone marrow transplant if she was going to live. Turns out Elizabeth was the best donor match. She agreed to donate, but she used that time to explore her relationship with Maggie.

"I guess it's what we do when we're threatened with the loss of someone. I did. My relationship with my son wasn't life or death in the same sense, but I stood a very real risk of losing our relationship forever way back then. So it's relevant. Loss is loss!"

Mike pushed his reading glasses back up his nose, picked up a page that looked torn out of a magazine and began to read. *"People have said I was brave to undergo the bone marrow harvest, but I don't think the procedure was so brave.*

Courage

What felt brave to me was that other kind of harvest and transplant, the soul marrow transplant, getting emotionally naked with another human being, putting aside pride and defensiveness, lifting the layers and sharing with each other our vulnerable souls.

"'She suffered so much. But she said life never tasted as sweet, and that's because of the soul-baring and the truth-telling we had done with each other. She became more unapologetically herself with everyone. She said things she'd always needed to say. She did things she always wanted to do. The same happened for me.'

"That is courage. That is what I went through with my son. That's what you can experience with yours if you are willing."

Alex looked down at his hands, silent.

"I'm willing," he said. "Scared, but willing." He took a deep breath. He was terrified actually, but he wasn't ready to admit that yet.

"Good," Mike paused. "I don't want to spoil the book for you, but one of the things her experience with her sister did was to radically change her. She became braver about being authentic with the people in her life. She spoke her own truths. She didn't stop with herself. She worked hard to draw out the core authenticity of those around her. Kind of like what we're doing.

"She wasn't fighting a great war or seeking to change the entire world. Isn't that what we as CEOs think our primary job is?" Mike laughed. "No, she focused on one key relationship in her life, and stood in courage to explore that relationship as deeply as she possibly could. In doing so, she learned an incredible amount about the vast reservoirs of strength within her and who she really was. She also learned how to be of service to others, and to help them find their best, most authentic selves.

"Elizabeth's situation was literally one of life and death. My situation with my son, your relationship with your son, they're nothing like this, but then they're everything like this. Being authentic means being vulnerable. It means emotional pain. It's a position we as men, and even women I suppose, fight hard not to get into—feeling pain, or feeling vulnerable or weak—but those are the very things that we use to define courage."

Alex shook his head and laughed, embarrassed. "I'm sorry. I'm still missing something," he admitted.

"Not a problem. Let me tell you another story then. It's nothing you or I will ever go through, and we may not be able to understand as men, but as parents I think we can relate.

"Rose Mapendo was an ordinary woman who showed extraordinary courage in the face of true horror. Rose was born in the Democratic Republic of Congo (then known as Zaire) in the early 1960s to a Tutsi family, one of many in the region who raised young women for marriage and motherhood. Rose never went to school and married when she was sixteen. In 1994, after giving birth to seven children, Rose and her husband moved to the city of Mbuji-Mayi to pursue better educational opportunities for their children. Rose's husband, in the meantime, began a new career as a butcher."

"Wait, wasn't that around the time of the Rwanda massacres? I was in college then. I remember the news," Alex said.

"Exactly," Mike said. "In April of that same year, conservative members of the Hutu-led government ordered mass killings of Tutsi families in neighboring Rwanda. More than 800,000 Tutsi were murdered in less than three months. For the next few years, the murders continued. By 1998, the Second Congo War had begun with the Democratic Republic of Congo in fierce battle against the Tutsi-led Rwandan government. Tutsis in Rwanda as well as the DRC were targeted for violence. My company was struggling with what to do with economic hits we were taking, while all this personal, microcosm stuff was playing out, unbeknownst to me at the time." Mike shook his head. "Horrible, horrible stuff."

"Did you know Rose?" Alex asked.

"No, but I heard about her story later. One of our offices there heard about her and wanted to donate money to her so she could leave and escape to the U.S.

"Before she even thought about the U.S., there were police officers visiting her over and over. They demanded to know about her husband's whereabouts and attempted to steal their money. Each time, Rose was able to convince them there was nothing there for them. She was also able to hide her husband. She thought they'd only take the men and leave the women and children alone. But she was wrong. The Hutu-backed government was willing to imprison, punish, and even kill all Tutsi, regardless of age or gender. Rose and her family began hiding in their own home, under the cover of darkness, rarely moving so as to not give away their location. However, in late September, Rose, her husband, and six of her children were taken prisoner with four other Tutsi families. But the worst of it had just begun.

"Life in the camp was horrific. The government ordered all the men to be murdered a week after Rose's family arrived. Two other women and two children were also killed in the process. Anyone not murdered was starved because they had little or no access to food and no health system. Lice were rampant; sanitation was nonexistent. Children and women defecated in the very cells in which they slept."

"That is so inhumane, I can't imagine," Alex said.

"Me neither."

Both men paused for a moment to reflect before Mike continued.

"So her husband was murdered. Then her son became the focus of the soldiers. He was almost an adult. To save her son's life, Rose had two choices: stand by and do nothing as a soldier murdered him, or offer a ransom. The only ransom she had at that time in the prison was her 17-year-old daughter. So she offered her as a sex slave to the soldier. "

"Oh my gosh," Alex dropped his head and shook it, imagining doing the same to save one of his children.

"Agreed. Rose made a choice that no mother should have to make. But it was one that helped save the lives of all her children, including the twins she was carrying at the time."

"Can it get worse?" Alex asked.

"It can, and it did," Mike said. "Rose gave birth to her twins on the dirty floor of the camp. She used a piece of wood and a thread tied in her hair to cut the umbilical cords. Once they were born, Rose made another difficult but incredible choice to ensure the survival of her family. She decided to forgive those who had harmed her and made this clear by naming her twins after two of the camp's commanders."

Mike leaned forward, placing both arms on the table, his hands clasped, his voice urgent. "Imagine the depth of fortitude and forgiveness Rose had to find inside herself to make that choice. Imagine the *courage*! Rose had just given one of her daughters as a sex slave to a soldier in order to save her son's life. That's not enough. What does she do next? She names her newborns after those who have committed unspeakable atrocities against her family and her tribe. That takes immense calmness and presence of mind, to say nothing of courage!

"Her strategy worked. According to the story we were told, the wife of one of the commanders soon visited with bread and clothing for Rose. And when orders came down for the rest of the prisoners in the camp to be executed, the commander had them transferred to another prison because he couldn't kill his namesake. It was at this prison that the soldier who held Rose's daughter visited the camp. Remembering Rose, he asked the son of the President of the DRC to not harm the family and to give them some money. Less than two weeks later, Rose and her children were released to a human rights center, then to an American aid center, and finally a Red Cross protection center in Cameroon by the U.S. government. That's when we heard about what she went through.

"All in all, Rose and her family were imprisoned for sixteen months. It was a lifetime for them, I'm sure."

"Horrific," Alex said. "And courageous. But other than me being a parent with children, it's not relevant to me."

"But it is," Mike said, slapping the table. "The story of Rose Mapendo isn't about war or corruption. It's about the power of great courage in the face of terrible odds. Rose could have allowed her impossible situation to defeat her and her family many times. She could have simply given up. But she chose to fight, and fight courageously, despite what little liberty she had. Considering where she was and the fact she chose to do what she did, how can any of us ever claim that our petty little struggles are 'too much'?"

Alex shrugged. "I guess you're right. Nothing my family has faced, or will ever face, God willing, will ever be that horrific."

Courage

"Oh, it didn't end there," Mike said. " In 2000, Rose and her children received refugee status and moved to the United States. Seven years later, Rose was also reunited with another daughter of hers she had thought was dead, the one she'd given to her relatives who managed to flee to Congo while Rose's family was taken prisoner. Though the road to reconciliation was rough, both Rose and her daughter forgave each other. Rose's daughter is now a wife and mother in her twenties, and is working as a caregiver."

"How do you know all this?" Alex asked.

"A documentary called 'Pushing the Elephant' was produced by PBS about the reunion of Rose and her daughter and followed them as they were getting to know one another and coming to terms with a painful past. It was about defining what it means to be a survivor, a woman, a refugee, and an American.

"Imagine living each day with a daughter whose mother had offered her as a sex slave. Here was a daughter who was given away to neighbors not knowing if she would ever see her again; a son who had been rescued from the jaws of death just before being shot in the head; twins whose names remind her everyday of the horrors she had been through. That my friend is courage.

"I remember I once saw an interview of this lady on TV, and when Rose was narrating her story, the reporter said, 'I can imagine what you might have gone through.' I still remember the pain and fortitude in her voice and the tears in her eyes when the camera zoomed in on her face as she asked the reporter, 'Can you?'

"Rose has dedicated her life since settling in America to bringing awareness to the violence plaguing women and children in the Democratic Republic of Congo. She regularly raises money to send to widows, prisoners and survivors of refugee camps.

"She organizes demonstrations to raise public awareness about the problems facing refugees around the world. Through a foundation established in her name, the Rose Mapendo Foundation, she provides survival resources to women in the DRC and surrounding areas who still face the threats of ethnic warfare every day.

"The mission of the Rose Mapendo Foundation is 'to empower the women of the Congo, Rwanda, and Burundi to work together, regardless of religious, tribal, or political differences, to achieve peace and reconciliation in the region.'

"Someone, a reporter I think, recently asked her about the difficulty of making tough decisions in the camp. Rose explained the power of courage:

'You have a choice. You can either quit and kill yourself or foster courage and say that there is a reason to have been put in that situation. And I made a decision to forgive the people who thought I was their enemy. And when I changed that, when I made the decision to forgive them, I became free from anger.'

***

"I know they're extreme stories, but sometimes that's the only way we can understand how powerful these pillars are. The media has watered down words like courage, honor, and hero so much that people just doing the right thing, like returning a wallet they find on the street, is called a 'hero.' I think we forget the roots and strength of true courage.

"Saying, or speaking, your truth is about taking ownership of who you are as a result of your experiences and your expressions. It stems from your core value system. The stronger your value system—the more you are passionate about your values—the more you take ownership of who you are. This, in turn, helps you create a steady path for growth. Lots of people may not like you, but this is your opportunity to create a stronger you. Moreover, leadership is not a popularity contest.

"The more ownership you take in yourself, the more trust you cultivate and the more success you have. Ownership is a critical part of this tenet. Saying your truth and taking ownership of yourself, your life, your situation, your actions and thoughts will help you become confident and develop your unique identity. 'Speak my truth' doesn't mean 'just speak and provide lip service.' it is actually living the truth with passion based on your values and your integrity.

Courage

"You take total ownership of your life, and live according to what you say you believe and how you're going to live. And what this means is that your values are nonnegotiable. You're not going to betray yourself or compromise your values.

"Be proud of who you are and believe in yourself. You should be the first person to believe in you. If you don't believe in yourself then you cannot expect others to believe in you. But it takes strength and courage to admit the truth and take ownership. Your truth is what you think impulsively, unapologetically, and unashamedly, so if you are not ashamed to think it, you should not be ashamed to say it, own it, and live it!

"Further, this passionate expression of who you are happens when you learn to be compassionate with yourself. Self-compassion forms the basis of what the Greeks, in all their wisdom, described as 'Arete' – a life of fulfillment, authenticity, and living to your full potential. Taking ownership means unapologetically admitting, 'I am not perfect, so do not expect perfection from me. I will make mistakes, but when I do make a mistake, I will own it and make amends, not excuses. I will tell you I am trying to improve.'

"Think about how you typically respond when someone asks you how you are doing. What do you usually say? If you're like most, you probably give some variation of the phrase 'I'm fine,' or 'Good!' But here's the key question: Do you really feel the way you say you do?

"I've found myself guilty of uttering the phrase 'I'm fine' to everyone, even close colleagues and family members. But that's just a socially-programmed response. It rarely tells others what you're really feeling or what you're dealing with in life. I think we internalize these responses so they become the "appropriate" social reactions that we have to get out of the way before we can get on to what we really want – a business conversation, a cup of coffee, discussions about the next family trip, or whatever."

"Guilty," Alex said. "I do the same thing. It's just less hassle. I don't have the time to get all touchy-feely or warm and fuzzy with everyone who asks me how I am."

"And most of them really don't want to hear it anyway!" Mike roared with laughter.

"But these questions and how we respond to them provide us with a real opportunity to say our truth and *take ownership* in small but enormously powerful ways," Mike continued. This is exactly what Elizabeth Lesser did with her sister. She decided she wouldn't give or take 'I'm fine' as an acceptable response. She wanted to take ownership of her life and create a bond with her sister that would enable both of them to grow. So she spoke her truth and asked her sister to do the same.

"As a result, they were both able to forge an incredible connection that allowed Elizabeth to tap into her authentic self and share that true self with others. I won't go into what I did with my son Mark just yet, but it started with our getting beyond that whole 'I'm fine' conversation. We got into some pretty brutally honest truths about our situation, our feelings, what was happening between us. We both had to take ownership of our feelings, our expectations, our anger. It was tough."

"You're saying truth and ownership go together?"

"Hell, yes. Here's the thing. We all have hard choices in life. You know what I mean—times when we have to choose between two right options or to pick the lesser evil between two wrong options. Our ability to make the best or right choice and act on it with conviction is what sets the courageous leader apart."

"That's not easy to do," Alex noted.

"No, it's not. Too many CEOs I know make the choice based on how the consequences will impact their bottom line or their career path, not on what's morally, ethically, and personally right," Mike said.

"So what should they do?"

"Well, we all need to strive for authenticity, even if it comes in a shape that we might not usually expect, or like. Speak your truth and stand up for what you truly believe in because if you say a word often enough, it becomes you.

"Say what you believe and say it with pride. Say it with dignity. Say it with authenticity because when you speak your mind consistently, you and those around you will begin to see a particular pattern emerging. You'll see what you value in life, what is important to you, what matters to you, and how you would like the world to know you, or how you would like to show up in life and those around you will see the same. Dr. Seuss said it very well, 'Say what you mean and mean what you say, for those who matter will not mind and those who mind don't matter.'

"If saying your truth is about taking ownership, standing up for what you believe is about holding yourself accountable for your actions and your ownership. These are related concepts, but accountability holds us to tough decisions. Accountability in any relationship means we stay true to our values and hope we become better people as a result. This is the beginning of you creating a life that follows your values. It evolves your identity and taps into your truthfulness to stimulate growth of character. In turn, all this accountability, honesty, and ownership creates an ecosystem for your personal growth as well as the growth of others around you.

"Both Elizabeth Lesser and Rose Mapendo found the courage to persevere in incredibly difficult circumstances by holding steady to their most cherished beliefs. Elizabeth loved her sister and wanted to connect with her on the deepest level possible. She made developing this bond with her sister a nonnegotiable condition of her bone marrow donation. She held herself accountable to this decision and stuck with it. Rose had to make the incredibly difficult decision to give her teenage daughter to a prison guard in order to spare her son's life, but she stuck to that choice because she knew it had the best chance of saving everyone in her family.

"I had to decide to tear down the very impenetrable walls I'd built around myself in order to let my son in. I risked my safety, and what I thought was my masculinity and strength and my entire worldview to get to what mattered most to me—my son's love and acceptance.

"The best choice in any circumstance is rarely the easiest one. But taking the time to discover your own values and truths does make taking a stand and holding yourself accountable somewhat easier. You see what needs to be done and you do it, as Elizabeth and Rose did. That doesn't mean you can't have doubts. In fact, doubt is a key way of testing how your values and actions align.

By standing up for what you believe and leaning into courage, you learn how to use doubt to your advantage and make the tough choices that will create the best opportunity for success.

"You've decided, or I think you've decided, that you'll do whatever you need to do to keep your son close. I don't think it's about ensuring that Adam runs your company or not. I think it's about creating and keeping a lifelong relationship. We're fathers. We want our children to be happy, successful, fulfilled, and to have a life better and easier than we did."

Alex leaned back in his chair, as if to distance himself from what Mike was saying. He fought the tenseness and the heart-clutching pain he was feeling just hearing Mike's words, let alone letting himself accept them. This was going to be tougher than he thought. He was afraid if he replied, he might cry. So he nodded, clenching his jaw as he did so to keep the tears from streaming.

Mike noticed his reaction. It was all hard to hear. He remembered that much. None of this happened overnight. It was going to be a long, hard journey. He hoped Alex was truly up for it. Nothing this powerful and valuable ever comes easy. But in the end it will all be worth it, he thought.

"Speaking our truth runs much deeper than speaking our opinions," Mike said gently. "Truth is about how we feel and what is real for us. It doesn't get any realer. Truth is not about being right. It's about expressing what we think and feel in an authentic, vulnerable, and transparent way.

"We speak our truth from a much deeper and more authentic place than we do our ideas or opinions. Speaking this deeper truth not only liberates us, but it has the potential to make a difference for others and bring us closer to those who matter to us. You may be wondering how you're going to speak your truth with Adam."

Alex nodded.

"He's in no mood to get into a serious discussion, let alone feel vulnerable with you. He's very busy protecting himself from you. The only way to help him let down his walls and put away his defensiveness is to show him you're not a threat. There are lots of things you can do to accomplish this. Begin by not trying to manage Adam's feelings. You probably come across very arrogant, condescending, and manipulative when you try to manage his feelings. You may believe you know how he feels about working with you, but actually you are being mean and hurtful to him by not letting him tell you what he truly feels or thinks.

"Second, and this is hard for us to do, stop thinking that just because you are his father you are right. You're not. I wasn't; you aren't. We need to be *real* and not *right* with our children. I can understand how passionate you are about ensuring that Adam takes on the mantle of your family business, but at the same time you will have to be more compassionate with him. He's sixteen. He's still developing. He doesn't have the world experience or cognitive capabilities to handle a lot of this yet.

"To be more compassionate, you will have to understand his perspective. And perspective-taking is not all that egotistically averse in a father-son relationship. It's really simple. It's simply looking at the world through Adam's eyes. Perspective-taking is one of the most important tools we have to be able to connect with others and expand our range of influence. When you take Adam's perspective and think about what he really wants, you're more likely to give him what he wants. This ensures you're more likely to achieve your goals. Start by giving Adam some options instead of directives. This will help him lower his guard and not be defensive.

"It's not easy. You'll need to practice, a lot. Don't worry. No matter how much you practice, you won't become perfect," Mike laughed as Alex rolled his eyes. "I've been practicing for decades, yet every time I talk to my son, I learn something new. Noticing everything that irritates you about others will make you a little more self-aware and a little more authentic if you don't let your emotions take over. Learn to be mindful of it, but not driven by it. Have empathy and compassion with yourself as you practice. This is not going to be easy, but believe me, it is going to be well worth it. It's not necessarily going to get easier.

In fact, it's always somewhat excruciating because each situation is always new and different. And, in your case with your your son, speaking up can be incredibly scary and challenging. Even if your legs shake, your voice quivers, or your heart races, all of which usually happens when we get real and vulnerable, don't back off. Take a deep breath, dig down for the smallest bit of courage you have within you, and be willing to speak your truth. In time, you'll start to see your relationship with your son and your lives literally transform. The most crucial thing right now for you is to stay connected to your son. Being vulnerable, honest, and courageous will help."

"Wow," Alex said, shaking his head. "I don't know if I can remember all that, let alone do it. Do you have a short-hand version?"

Mike nodded. "I do. "You will need to open your heart and tell Adam, 'This is my truth and I have to tell it to you so I stay connected to you. So it's not about whether you make amends or heed to my advice. This isn't about whether I get what I need from you to stay in relationship with you. This is about you staying connected to me and that hopefully you value me enough as I speak from the vulnerability of my truth to somehow rise up, step up, match my vulnerability, and engage in a discussion with me so that we can move forward.'

"We often think of vulnerability as a weakness, or a condition to be overcome. This is especially true in the business world, where vulnerability equates to the possibility of financial loss, corporate take over, or defeat by competitors seeking advantages in the marketplace. It's true as men, too. We have a whole other mess to deal with when it comes to emotions and vulnerability. But vulnerability plays a key role in how we maintain fruitful relationships with others. In fact, being vulnerable is perhaps the biggest requirement in developing that connection in the first place.

"Think back to any relationship you've developed in your life that you would consider significant, deep,or meaningful to you as a person. Did you open yourself to that person and show a side of you that most others hadn't seen? What did that exposure feel like? How was the other person open to you? Did you accept their openness, in turn, and reciprocate mutual trust?

"I remember when I started dating. I wanted the girl to like me, so I opened up a bit, bragged a bit maybe." Both men laughed. "It was when I really started being honest about my feelings with her that I started to get that rush we call

Courage

'love.' Maybe it was love, eventually, but looking back I can see that it was really the excitement that comes with risk and being vulnerable. I think that's the first step to love, or bonding and connecting with another. For me that's what significant relationships feel like—that rush of opening one's self to another, that freefall of trust.

"Let me tell you something about the next important tenet. Passion. Philosopher Dan Dennett once said, 'Find something more important than you are, and dedicate your life to it.' Growing up, what was your passion?" Mike asked. This was a curveball that Alex was not expecting, and he hadn't given his passions a second, or even first, thought in a long, long time.

Even so, Alex didn't have to think long. He said, "I have always wanted to be the best at whatever I do. I wanted to make it big in the corporate world. I come from a humble background, and at a young age, I had decided that I would do something that would earn me a lot of respect, money, and prestige."

"I'm glad you mention prestige," Mike said. "You failed at that."

Alex looked up, startled. "What do you mean I failed?"

"If you were only seeking prestige, you wouldn't be where you are today. Prestige is a dangerous trap. If you were just hooked on prestige, you wouldn't be able to follow your passion. Passion is something that you completely immerse yourself in. When you follow your heart, you throw prestige out the window. You were ambitious, and hence, you made it big, not because you wanted prestige. That is what you are perhaps trying with Adam. You want him to do something befitting your own prestigious status in the corporate world, and you are not getting to the root of his ambition—his passion." Alex was struck dumb by Mike's brutal honesty.

"The root of courage is vulnerability. Imperfection is perfection. Once you embrace vulnerability, you have exposed yourself. It gives you strength. It opens you to others. It helps you connect more strongly with others."

"I admit, I'm not big on the vulnerability thing at all," Alex confessed. "My wife, well, my first wife left me over that. Adam's mother is more tolerant because she's not exactly vulnerable herself."

"And I'm guessing Adam struggles with that as well."

"He does. He's very reluctant to share any of his life with us. And we're both desperate to hear what's really going on with him."

"Yet," Mike said, "You're not willing to be vulnerable or open with him about yourselves."

"Bingo." Alex shook his head. "How stupid are we? Why did I not see that?"

"Most of us don't. We want to stay behind the safe walls we've built for ourselves and let others take the risks. Then, like you and me, we wonder why others don't want to talk to us.

"You know, a few years ago, Brené Brown discussed the power of vulnerability in one of the most-viewed and highly-rated TED Talks of all time. She talked about 'whole hearted' people, people who lived from a deep sense of worthiness. She wanted to find out what separated them from people who struggled to find a sense of worthiness in their lives. What she found was, one, that 'whole hearted' people had the courage to be imperfect, and two, *they fully embraced their vulnerability*. In fact, Brown said, 'They believed that what made them vulnerable made them beautiful.' And they believed their vulnerability was absolutely necessary for them to live a courageous life.

"I didn't believe it years ago, but I agree with her now. She believes human beings are 'wired for struggle.' In other words, we *have* to face fears, problems, tough choices, and vulnerable moments to be the humans we are meant to be. Those who are wholehearted have learned to embrace these struggles, to live completely in vulnerability, because they know it will make their lives—and everyone's life they touch—immeasurably richer and more beautiful. When we learn to work from a place of vulnerability and acceptance, we demonstrate the courage to exist as our authentic selves and encourage the same in others."

"Damn. That's a scary thought!" Alex said.

"It's even scarier in practice! You will need to let Adam into your life a bit as well as help him find his passion. You know, Alain de Botton, a British author and philosopher, says something I totally agree with. He said that we think we know what success is, and we often try to force it onto others, especially our children."

"My father did the same with me," Alex said. "He thought he knew what I wanted, but he didn't. I'm doing the same with Adam."

Mike nodded. "You do it because you love him. But love means letting him find his passion. You're a CEO. You know that work fills the largest part of our lives. That's going to be true for Adam, too, but he will need to love his work passionately. He needs to have extreme clarity about what he wants to do and immerse himself in it totally. His passion needs to be a part of his DNA, so he is in complete *flow* when he works. Now let me ask you something," Mike said.

"Of course."

"Have you ever heard the word 'prudence'?"

"Sure, from my grandmother. Wow! That's a blast from the past. I haven't heard that word in decades."

"Do you know what it means?"

Alex shrugged. "Being cautious, taking your time, making smart decisions, I guess."

"Close. Prudence is a virtue, actually considered to be the 'mother of all virtues' by both the ancient Greeks and most Christian philosophers. Derived from the Latin word *prudentia*, meaning 'foresight and sagacity,' it signals wisdom, specifically the wisdom needed to govern oneself appropriately by the use of reason. Prudence is deeply linked to courage. Deciding when an action is courageous, rather than reckless or wanton, is considered a virtuous act of prudence.

"We may not think much about it, but prudence is an incredibly strong balancing force against power exercised wrongly over others. Think about Rose Mapendo. She was imprisoned in a camp with her family, held against her will, and had no power to control her situation in any way. But Rose *did* have prudence. She knew how to engage adversaries and when to act with patience and fortitude to make decisions—however difficult—that would yield the results she was seeking. Those who had power over her ultimately had no control over how she lived her life.

"This is the big lesson of prudence over power. Prudence gives you control over yourself. Power gives you control over others. Control over yourself is always more powerful than control over others.

"I'd agree with that," Alex said.

Mike got up from the table and motioned to Alex.

"Come with me." The two men went inside and across the living room to Mike's library and his extensive collection of books. As Mike moved back and forth, pulling out books and looking for a specific book, he said, "I remember I once met a former head of state in Singapore. We had a very interesting discussion. He gave me a book he had written, and when I asked him about the leadership challenges he had faced as the head of an Asian country, he showed me this page."

Mike pulled his reading glasses out, put them on, and then flipped through the pages. He began to read, "'Underlying any leader's analysis has to be keen awareness that on his decision hangs the fate of millions of people and the future of his country. It is at times like these that the leader is confronted by his acute loneliness. He may listen to any amount of advice he chooses, but at the end of the day, the decision has to be his alone. He realizes then that the buck really stops with him.' This is no facile cliche.

"I was working on my COVETed leader model at that time, so I asked him, 'Wouldn't this be true of anyone who wanted to show up as a COVETed leader in life? The stakes may not be that high, but the principle would be the same.'"

"What did he say?" Alex asked.

Mike smiled and said, "After I explained the concept to him, he agreed. Would you agree that prudence, courage, vulnerability, all those tenets we just discussed, require two things we both crave and hate?"

"And those would be?"

"The ability to accept criticism and to give candid feedback."

"The two most dreaded conversations in my world," Alex joked.

"They were mine, too, for a while. Now they're the two things I value most. We have to have the ability to give and accept genuine feedback from others. This happens in annual reviews and guided meetings, of course, but it does

Courage

and should happen in life all around us—from friends, family, even strangers. If we are truly honest and authentic with ourselves, we can see the areas we could improve and the places where we could be better, more giving, and more courageous.

"Hearing that others see those same areas in us can be embarrassing or discouraging, but we have to do it to become our best. Being authentic with ourselves in order to grow demands we give those we care about the same courtesy in honest feedback so they can grow."

"But not everyone wants that candid feedback," Alex said. "In fact, most don't. Employees, my family, friends. They all want to hear the soft version, the cheerleader version, where I cheer them on and ignore their faults and weaknesses. It's like a game we play where we all stick our heads in the sand and promise to ignore the faults in each other. In fact, even I was completely pissed when you were so blatantly honest with your feedback."

"How's that working for you?" Mike smiled.

"It's not."

"I didn't think so. You know, giving and receiving candid feedback is a skill that requires courage. And when you are candid in your feedback you can make difficult conversations less painful. You will totally transform the relationship into one of authenticity, and most importantly, set the ground for real and lasting changes. One critical aspect of that skill is agility," Mike explained.

"Agile like fast and flexible, or agile like in software management?"

Mike thought for a moment.

"Both," he said.

"You can *only* give candid feedback if you're agile—meaning fast and flexible—and divide your feedback into short phrases with frequent reassessment and adaptation of your feedback. Great leaders check in on performance and learning goals and support the people they lead as their challenges shift over time. It also requires *you* to be nimble when your own goals and challenges change.

"The ability to move quickly, easily, courageously, and *authentically* through the process of a feedback exchange allows us to connect more deeply with the people who seek our guidance. By the way, learning agility is an important part of any successful leader. It is a willingness to relentlessly learn that makes us grow intellectually, socially, and spiritually. Self-growth is based on our mental model of being willing to engage in self-reflection and to become more self-aware."

***

Alex thought for a minute, absorbing the new concepts he had just learned. Courage was clearly an important quality for anyone to have. Just look at Elizabeth Lesser and Rose Mapendo. But how could business leaders cultivate these same qualities in themselves and inspire those they lead to do the same?

Alex voiced these questions. Mike leaned back and studied him before responding.

"I think you may benefit from hearing the opposite perspective. What about a leader who *lacks* the courage to do the right thing? Or one who punishes others for demonstrating it?

"I've got another story for you. But I'm only going to tell you half of it right now. You'll hear the rest when you're ready, once you've learned all you can from my COVET system of leadership."

Alex laughed. "Fair enough! I love a good cliffhanger. Let's hear it."

"Years ago, many, many years ago—only five or so years out of college—I worked as an executive assistant for the CEO of another large manufacturing company. He knew my father, and they worked out something that put me on a fast track to management. I was very fortunate as I was forced to learn things quickly.

"This CEO was known for being very successful in his business affairs, but he defied every definition of a great leader. I mean he was terrible at creating positive relationships with his employees, and he rarely, if ever, tried to encourage them or develop their talents. He was arrogant, rude, dismissive, and extremely short-tempered, particularly with those he viewed as being beneath him.

Courage

"One day, a company driver who often transported the CEO to various meetings accidentally dropped him off at the wrong location. It was an honest mistake. The driver routinely brought the CEO to this place for meetings. He had simply gotten confused about the schedule. The real location was too far away to reach in time, so the CEO would be unable to attend.

"The CEO was furious. He was an important person! He was supposed to lead the meeting! How would anything get done without him? In his eyes, the driver was an idiot, a moron, incompetent, and incapable of making his important life easier. So he shouted at the driver until he was red in the face. And then he took the car, leaving the driver stranded far away from the company offices.

"Later that day, I received a phone call from the CEO. He fumed about what had happened and demanded I fire the driver. Respectfully, I told the CEO I disagreed with his decision and asked him to reconsider. But he was unmoved.

"The next day, I called the driver to my office. I told him the situation and what the CEO had asked me to do. I said, 'I'm sorry. I don't agree with the CEO, but this is what I have been instructed to do. What do you think?'

"He said, 'Sir, I believe you. I know you. I know you very well. You wouldn't do anything inappropriate.'

"I said, 'I can still fight for you. I can stand up for you.'

"He responded, 'No sir. I'm a driver. I can find another driver's position somewhere else. Why do you want to jeopardize your career?' I was stunned by his willingness to support *me*. He was the wronged party! And yet here he was, exhibiting the tenets of courage in one simple act: perspective-taking, embracing his vulnerability, teaching me a lesson in doing so, and exercising prudence instead of getting bitter and reproachful. He was even offering me candid feedback by questioning why I would give up my career for his!

"We hugged each other. He left with tears in his eyes and I left with tears in my eyes. Mine were tears of regret while his were tears of compassion. It was a tough day.

"Later, I went to the CEO and said, 'This is not on my conscience. I don't believe in or agree with what you chose. I've carried out your orders, but I don't agree with you. This is on your conscience, not mine.' Was I afraid? No. Rather, I had learned something from the driver. It was important to share my belief that the CEO had done something wrong. I had to say my truth, which I did, but I also learned to be prudent.

"I also told my boss, 'I am paying the driver extra.' I had given him an extra month's salary in a small gesture of appreciation for his sacrifice. I felt it was the least I could do.

"To this day, I still carry the guilt that I fired him and obeyed orders instead of listening to my conscience.

"I learned several important lessons that day. But the company CEO would encounter this man again, and learn a far greater truth about his COVETed self in the process."

***

Mike stopped and leaned back in his chair. Alex, tense and sitting forward, let out a sharp laugh.

"What? That's it? Now I really want to know what happens next! How would he ever encounter that guy again? And did he ever change his attitude?"

Mike smiled. "You'll have to wait and see. Homework first. Next month, we'll move on to the next pillar: Optimism."

IN SUMMARY:

The first pillar of The COVETed Leader is Courage: the ability to select between two rights and act on it with conviction or to differentiate between two wrongs and say it is so.

Courage is all about leadership, about building a leader's demeanor and showing up with passion—to be able to 'say your truth,' being passionate about your beliefs and your values, and taking complete ownership of who you are, your experiences, and showing compassion, not only towards others but also towards yourself.

The only non-transferable asset you have is 'You.' The appreciation or depreciation of the value of this asset is not market dependent. It is self dependent.

The five tenets of Courage are:

- **Say your truth.** Speaking up and speaking your truth is an essential aspect of taking ownership for who you are and what has happened to you. Instead of blaming others, blaming circumstances, and being bitter, take responsibility for what you have done, or failed to do. Courage is an unapologetic way of living an authentic life based on nonnegotiable values, integrity, and authenticity.

    Even when it's difficult, challenging, politically incorrect, or politically unwise, speak your truth because you are absolutely clear about your passions. The right thing to do or say is rarely the easy thing to do or say. Many of us remain silent when speaking up would stop, change, or even derail what is happening in front of us, be it gossip, imprudent company policy, a demand from someone (supervisor or coworker) to do something illegal or unethical.
- **Stand up for what you believe.** If you truly believe in something, stand up for it. Set boundaries for yourself, and hold yourself firmly accountable to them. When we believe strongly enough in something to stand up for it, we are being true to our beliefs. We have them because we've chosen them, and they define our identity. Those who believe things because others have told them to, suffer from approval addiction and will rarely stand up for that thing if they're threatened with loss or sanctions.
- **Embrace vulnerability.** Vulnerability is the deep expression of your most sacred thoughts, opinions, and feelings—the things others could use against you if they chose to. The degree of your vulnerability is the extent of your willingness to share yourself with others, authentically and without apology for who you are.

Vulnerability is about exposing your flaws, secrets, and your weaker and darker sides without shame. But the strength you derive from embracing vulnerability and accepting your imperfections will become the source of long-lasting connectedness and exponential growth.

- **Prudence over Power.** Prudence is the ability to govern oneself through the use of reason. It is considered the measure of exercising moral authority and patience since it's based on ethical standards. Power is simply the ability to do something with force or strength, regardless of reason, morals, or ethics. COVETed leaders act with prudence and patience.

  They avoid using the power of their position for reproach. They believe in making others feel bigger and better than who they think they are. They are able to tame their egos and engage adversaries when in positions of power.

- **Accept criticism and give candid feedback.** One of the most challenging skill sets leaders must develop is the ability to accept criticism and give feedback when they interact, engage, and lead their followers. One of the most critical traits of a COVETed leader is to remain nimble and agile, the ability to develop mental, physical, emotional, social, and learning agility. It is extremely important for a leader to be able to learn relentlessly.

Chapter Four

OPTIMISM

"I love all that you had to say about Courage," Alex said. He hesitated. "You're going to say that a person would have to be a real optimist to believe that there is that much courage in the world, let alone in a person." Mike laughed. "You're right. That is why Optimism is the second pillar of the COVETed leader model.

"Let me tell you about a woman I heard about when I was in Africa years ago. I actually met this woman once after hearing her speak. Her story is amazing. She embodies the definition of the word 'Optimism'.

"Her name is Wangari Maathai. She passed away in 2011, but her passion and the things she believed so strongly in live on to this day. She was born in the central highlands of Kenya, in what is called the Nyeri District. Her father worked as a farmhand on rural, white-owned farms, which often did not offer schools for children.

"So, at the age of eight the Maathai children and their mother moved to a small village where Wangari began her formal schooling at the Ihithe Primary School. Later, she attended the only Catholic high school for girls in Kenya, Loreto High School, and in 1960, she became one of 300 Kenyans selected to study in the United States, supported by the Joseph P. Kennedy Jr. Foundation. In fact, Wangari would become the first woman in East and Central Africa to earn a doctorate degree.

"At the University of Pittsburgh, where she studied biology in a master's program, she first experienced the power of environmental restoration. Wangari witnessed local environmentalists running a grassroots campaign to rid the city of air pollution. She saw the possibilities for positive environmental change by the people themselves. After moving to Nairobi to earn her doctorate in veterinary anatomy, she taught at the University of Nairobi and became involved in a number of civic organizations and activist causes for women's and environmental rights.

"She decided to solve environmental issues by addressing some of the deep socioeconomic issues that plagued her people in Kenya.

"The rising unemployment rate in Kenya gave Wangari the idea to connect environmental restoration to providing jobs for the unemployed. She founded a business called Envirocare Ltd. that helped ordinary people plant trees to conserve the environment. She was able to plant her first nursery, but the business ultimately failed. She remained optimistic that her plan would ultimately succeed.

"On June 5, 1977 – World Environment Day – Wangari led the National Council of Women of Kenya (NCWK) in a march through Nairobi to the outskirts of the city. Here, they planted seven trees in honor of historical community leaders. That march was the beginning of what would become known as The Green Belt Movement.

"The Green Belt Movement, as Wangari envisioned it, began with a simple idea: women living in rural communities could make serious cultural, economic, and environmental change through the simple act of planting a tree. Many of these women reported to Wangari and the NCWK that streams in their communities were drying up, their food supplies were dwindling, and firewood had to come from further and further away.

"The Green Belt Movement encouraged women to work together to grow tree seedlings and helped them plant full-grown trees that would store rainwater and provide firewood and food. In exchange, the women received a small monetary stipend that allowed them to purchase food and goods to stimulate economic growth.

"With this program, Wangari and the NCWK did much more than help women plant trees. They instilled a sense of hope and optimism in rural communities that had long seen their natural resources dwindle and taken away.

"Wangari extended this program to several small communities around Nairobi. But soon, she began to realize that the environmental issues they faced – namely, environmental degradation, food insecurity, and deforestation – were actually caused by deeper social and cultural issues. Disempowerment and disenfranchisement were the norm rather than the exception. Moreover, most communities felt the loss of their traditional values that had allowed them to protect their environment in solidarity and trust with other local communities.

"Seeing this, Wangari helped The Green Belt Movement organize seminars in environmental and, soon, civic education. They are now called Community Empowerment and Education (CEE) seminars, and their main goal is to help individuals understand why they lacked the agency and power to change not only their environmental circumstances, but also their political and economic situations. The Green Belt Movement also began to advocate for greater democratic space and more accountability from local leaders. As the movement spread throughout the country, those involved began to hold national leaders to greater levels of accountability as well.

"Today, The Green Belt Movement continues to plant trees and educate local communities on the ways in which they can improve their environmental and socioeconomic conditions. In addition, they fight against land grabbing and the encroachment of agriculture into protected forest land. They contest building projects that demonstrate a lack of good faith in respecting local environmental and cultural customs, and they promote democracy and poverty reduction among those who are most disenfranchised, especially women. Finally, they advocate for the release of political prisoners. They've even extended their reach internationally, joining forces with other environmental organizations to campaign on behalf of climate change, deforestation, and "reduce, reuse, recycle" initiatives around the globe.

"All of this began from a simple, positive premise, and from the mind of one optimistic individual. Wangari was not a top political figure; nor was she a well-known environmental researcher when she began this project. But what she lacked in connections or fame, she more than made up for in optimism. Wangari never gave up. More importantly, she remained upbeat, calm, and confident in her project and the many ways it could benefit the women of Nairobi. Indeed, Wangari saw her work as optimistic and altruistic at its core. She said, 'We cannot tire or give up. We owe it to our present and future of all species to rise up and walk.'

"Wangari would go on to win the Nobel Peace Prize in 2004 for her work creating and developing The Green Belt Movement. Her legacy lives on through the Wangari Maathai Institute for Peace and Environmental Studies (WMI), an organization that brings together academic research on land use, forestry, agriculture, resource-based conflicts, and peace studies with The Green Belt Movement approach and membership base.

"Wow!" Alex exclaimed. "Impressive. One person could develop a global movement that impacts so many? But what if I want to start smaller? How do I create optimism where there isn't any?"

"Well," said Mike, "Optimism isn't a hard-and-fast condition. Think of it instead as a belief, a state of mind. If something has to happen in your life, believe that it will. If it doesn't happen, then something better will manifest. You have to reposition your mind and embrace the positivity. Let me illustrate this with another story, this one a little smaller in scope.

"In 2006, a journalist named Becky Blanton was living in a 1975 Chevy van in a Denver, Colorado, Walmart parking lot with her pets, a dog and a cat. She was homeless, but not without hope. She became homeless after after her father died when she quit her job to travel. Her plan was to freelance her photography and writing and explore the western United States. When she lost her only freelancing job and couldn't find another, she got a job working full-time in Denver and started hunting for an apartment. She couldn't find any housing that she could afford on a minimum wage job. So she continued to live in the van, to work full-time, and to hunt for an apartment.

"Living in the van didn't bother her. But having coworkers and everyone she encountered treat her as a "homeless woman" with all the stereotypical reactions was devastating to her. I asked her about her experience, about all the

Optimism

bullying, the negative responses, the lack of support, no friends. Her life wasn't anything that would cause someone to be optimistic. But she was.

"'I got through it by believing tomorrow would always be a better day, and by thanking God every day for what I did have, and not thinking about what I didn't have,' she said. 'I remembered some sales training I'd had once. The instructor told us we would hear the word *No* more than we would hear the word *Yes*. In fact, he said on average we'd hear 20 to 60 *No's* for every *Yes* we got. He said, "Every time you hear the word *No* you should get excited. It means you're that much closer to a *Yes*." As each day would pass, with whatever trouble, stress and trauma it had, I would get excited and tell myself, "You're one day closer to the most fantastic day of your life."'

"And was she?" Alex asked.

"Well, after 18 months, she got a job, found an apartment, and got off the streets." Mike said.

"That's good, but I wouldn't call it fantastic."

"Well, that's not the whole story, Mike continued. "She got sick. Her cat died. She lost her job, and moved back into her van a year later. Then her van broke down as she left town so she was forced to sleep in a parking lot in a sketchy area off the highway. She told me that as she drifted off to sleep, she told herself, 'You're one day closer to the most fantastic day of your life.' She was thankful she had a van to sleep in, a comfortable bed, a cell phone, and contacts in the area who might help her.

"The next day she called a business owner she had interviewed for a newspaper story months before she got sick. She was in his area of the state and asked him for the name of a good mechanic. Instead of giving her a name, he drove an hour out to where she was and fixed the van himself, and gave her fifty dollars to help her on her way.

"With that fifty`, she was able to get to the next town and sleep in another Walmart parking lot. Again, she told herself, 'You're one day closer to the most fantastic day of your life, and she thanked God for the fixed van, food, her dog, everything she could think of to make her feel grateful, focusing on what she had, not on what she didn't have. The next morning a woman she'd met in a social media group online called her. She asked her if she'd be willing to housesit for her and take care of her for a month while she recovered from back surgery. She'd provide room and board for her. She agreed. Now she had food, a place to stay, and a job.

"Meanwhile, she heard from the TED speaker's committee. She had won a writing contest the year before. First prize was a trip to Oxford, England, to attend the conference."

"That was the most fantastic day of her life!" Alex exclaimed.

"Not yet," Mike smiled. "The TED committee had asked all conference attendees, around 600, to submit a story about their experience on 'being invisible.' A handful of them would be selected to speak at the conference."

"She was selected."

"Yes. She was selected, and she spoke at the 2009 TED Global conference at Oxford University in Oxford, England. It was the first time she'd ever spoken in public, and it was the most fantastic day of her life, all because she had been optimistic all along, believing that a fantastic day beyond her ability to conceive it would happen. 'Optimism,' she told me, 'is like a candle. The darker the room, or the darker the night, the brighter the candle is. The worse things are, the more important it is to believe that something better is about to happen in your life. If something I desperately wanted didn't happen, I would trust that God had something better in mind for me and that whatever that was, it was on its way. It always was.

"'We have a choice,' she said. 'We can believe the worst is about to happen, or we can believe the best is about to happen. The odd thing is, what you believe in, good or bad, is what you get. Knowing that, why wouldn't I choose to believe the best was yet to be?'

"She took her experience, started her own ghostwriting business, and today she has a non-profit charity where she teaches homeless people to start their own businesses, but more importantly, she teaches them the power of optimism."

"Wow!" Alex poured himself another glass of tea and sat back. "That's an amazing story, too."

Optimism

"It is. But more amazing are the lessons it has to offer," Mike said.

"Such as?"

"First, a lesson about belief. Everything happens for a reason and a purpose. Even if something doesn't turn out how you wanted it to, you take that as a learning experience and imagine the possibilities of improvement. What did you learn? How can I improve this situation? There are no failures in life, only lessons."

"Isn't that just blind faith? What can you learn from being homeless?" Alex asked.

"A lot. In her TED talk, she explains that a friend called her one night to tell her that an essay she had written had just been published in a book. She went to the nearest bookstore, found the book, and read her essay. It had been chosen out of 60,000 entries, and was the number one essay in the book."

"What book?"

"*Wisdom of Our Fathers, Letters from Sons and Daughters,* by Tim Russert, the late Senior Vice President of NBC News, and the longest running moderator of the show, 'Meet the Press.' She said she stood in the bookstore to read it because she couldn't afford to buy the book. As she stood there and read the essay, something inside her changed. She said it was like lightning struck something inside her. She told herself, 'I'm not homeless. I'm a writer!' For months, she'd forgotten who she was, what her passion was. Rereading what she had written long ago reminded her.

"Understanding who she really was, and realizing she was not who people told her she was, changed her life. The lesson, she said, was that she learned that you can't let other people define you. You have to discover and hold fast to who you are or you're lost. 'The only asset,' she said, 'that was not transferable was *You*. The appreciation or depreciation of the value of this asset is not market driven but self driven.'

"She was, and is still, a writer. Since TED, she's gone to Africa twice, ghost-written two best-selling books, and traveled extensively around the country writing. 'You have to believe, in your God, your faith, yourself, and in the truth that tomorrow will be the most fantastic day of your life,' she said. Optimism is such a personal thing, and yet it's such a powerful force if we embrace it."

"And the other lesson?" Alex asked.

"Perhaps that is the most important one—that just as you can't have a blazing candle without the darkness around it, you can't be optimistic in an environment where everything is going well. To be optimistic you must be in a situation where things are going badly. Optimism is the gift tragedy and bad times bring us. It's like we can't get a rainbow without the rain first."

"So the lesson is to welcome hard times?"

"Something like that," Mike said. "But only if you want to be a COVETed leader."

Alex nodded his head vigorously. "I do. But how can I welcome hard times when I find it difficult to feel any kind of optimism at all? How do you create optimism when there isn't any to begin with?"

Mike laughed. "At a certain point, you just have to start! Remember what Becky told me, 'We all have a choice. We can either believe in the worst or the best, and go from there. What you believe in is what you will get in return.' She chose to believe the best was yet to come. And she developed that mindset using one sentence: You're one day closer to the most fantastic day of your life.

"Becky's story really exemplifies all the tenets of optimism: an attitude of gratitude, a belief in people, positivity, a can-do attitude, and the creativity and innovation that kept her moving forward. By practicing these tenets, you too can cultivate the belief that if something has to happen, it will happen, and if it doesn't, then something better will happen.

"It all starts with gratitude. Tell me, what was the most remarkable part of Becky's story to you?"

Alex thought for a minute. "Well, to me, the most remarkable thing about it was her focus on the good over the bad. I mean, at certain times, she had so little! But she was always grateful for what she did have. It was like she said; better and better things did happen."

"Exactly," Mike said. "You know, Plato was a great philosopher, and one of his greatest observations was 'a grateful mind is a great mind which eventually attracts to itself great things.' It might just seem like an observation by him, but recent scientific studies show that people who are more grateful and kind have higher levels of well-being and are happier, less depressed, less stressed, and more satisfied with their lives and social relationships.

"The simple act of expressing gratitude leads to other kinds of positive emotions, such as enthusiasm and inspiration, because it promotes the savoring of positive experiences. Gratitude gives you the emotional courage to feel and embrace the *full* spectrum of emotional experience, both positive and negative. It stems from self-acceptance, coupled with a willingness to move outside your comfort zone, to explore new ways of being that may not be familiar.

"Ultimately gratitude helps people optimize feelings of enjoyment, no matter what their circumstances are. Gratitude is ultimately a quest for self-realization and fulfillment. It uproots the sources of fear that result in anxiety, worry, sorrow, and depression that poison the proverbial wellspring of joy."

"You mean just being grateful can change your emotions?" Alex asked. He wasn't sure why, but his eyes began to tear up thinking about how ungrateful he was for all he had.

"According to studies, yes, it can. It also gives you a better understanding and awareness of your thoughts, and it makes you conscious of your emotions. You know, according to recent research by the Department of Neuroscience and Psychology at the University of Glasgow, there are only four basic emotions: Fear, Anger, Sorrow and Joy," Mike said, trying to distract Alex from the thoughts he appeared to be having.

"Those are all broad emotions. And they're powerful," Mike said. "I believe that gratitude gives you a sort of emotional courage that can become an antidote to fear, but let's look at all four in more detail.

"Let's start with Fear. You know what they say about fear right? It's an acronym for *False Evidence Appearing Real*. Your fear about losing Adam is absolutely baseless, and I will prove that to you. But first, let me explain what true fear is. By definition, fear is an unpleasant or even terrifying emotion caused by the belief or the thought that someone or something is dangerous, and likely to cause pain, harm, or loss. Fear can range from thinking someone will reject us or not like us all the way up to the fear we feel when we think there's an intruder in our house.

"There's fear of the unknown, of scarcity, loss. But fear is always about something in the future. The Dalai Lama once said, 'There are only two days in the year that nothing can be done. One is called Yesterday and the other is called Tomorrow. Today is the right day to Love, Believe, Do and mostly Live.'"

Alex clenched his lips together. He hated to admit it to Mike, but he lived in fear. It wasn't something that came up every once in awhile. It was persistent, relentless. He was afraid of failing, of not being able to provide, of making the wrong decision, saying the wrong thing, doing the wrong thing. How do you deal with that kind of fear?

Mike looked at him and nodded once, as though he could hear Alex's thoughts. "Then there's that daily, relentless fear that's as much a part of our lives as breathing. You know, the fear that you're not good enough, or that you're going to make a mistake and bring this big house of cards crashing down all around you.

"Alex, fear and anxiety are actually necessary for our survival. Everybody experiences fear, even the bravest and the most courageous leaders in history have admitted to having to change their underwear a time or two."

Alex laughed. "Yeah, I get that."

"Mahatma Gandhi, Martin Luther King, Jr., and Nelson Mandela, some of my favorite leaders by the way, talk about instances in their lives when fear was absolutely overwhelming, and reflecting back on those moments made them wonder how they got through those times. Those moments are so important they write about them in their biographies and share them in speeches. It's how they reassure us they're not immune to fear.

"I remember I read somewhere that Nelson Mandela was once traveling in a jet, and to his surprise, he noticed that one of the propellers was not working. He looked through the window and was shocked to see that the propeller had actually stopped. He then casually turned to his bodyguard and told him about it.

Optimism

The bodyguard panicked and rushed to the cockpit to alert the pilots who were already aware of the situation and were dealing with it. After grappling with the emergency for almost an hour, the plane landed safely, and luckily there was no mishap. Once on the ground, the bodyguard came up to Mandela and mentioned that he had seemed pretty casual about it. He asked if he had been scared. Mandela said, 'Man, I was terrified up there.' He hadn't shown it, but he certainly felt it.

"So regardless of who someone is, or what they appear to feel or not feel, we all experience fear. Courage is not necessarily the absence of fear. It is the ability to deal with it without letting it cripple or disable you.

"Mandela was able to see the propeller, alert his guard, and then wait for the pilots to fix it without adding to the fear of those around him by acting fearful. His calmness, I'm guessing, helped the situation by calming others. Being able to feel fear, and stay calm and composed, is actually a sign of wisdom. Don't hold onto fear – it's toxic energy. You don't need to fight or ignore fear either. When you learn to recognize it and deal with it, you can release it and set yourself free from its power."

Alex nodded and sipped his tea before replying. "How do you release fear?"

"By recognizing it and understanding it."

"I don't get it," Alex said. "I know what it feels like, but how do I understand it?"

"Well, fear manifests in many ways. It could show up as *shame*, a feeling of wanting to become invisible, a desperate need to hide, to want to disappear, to pretend you never existed because you feel defective."

Alex was nodding and smiling as Mike talked.

"Got it. You feel like you're not enough, inferior. You're not meeting your family's or your employee's expectations. You're a total failure, not good enough, not perfect enough."

It was Mike's turn to nod. "We've all been there. We've all felt that, Alex. You're not alone."

"I wish it were just *sometimes*. I could handle feeling that way once in awhile. I just hate feeling it all the time."

"What do you mean?" Mike asked.

"I know I'm this big deal CEO, the man with the world on his shoulders, calling the shots, making the decisions and appearing successful, but most of the time I just want to disappear and pretend that I never existed. Then, when I see Adam and David, I think, there goes the reason for my existence, and I feel life is worth living. But, if I am not able to keep Adam close, keep him happy, keep him feeling safe and protected, then I ask myself, why all this effort? Why all this struggle?"

"So who are you trying to protect, Adam or yourself?" Mike asked.

"I don't know."

"Well," said Mike, "Fear has a second component: guilt. Guilt is feeling like we need to fix something – a wrongdoing, a bad choice, or a bad behavior. We feel responsible for something we've done, something that is either morally wrong or inappropriate. Maybe we let somebody down, or hurt their feelings, or really ruined someone's life in some way.

"We can feel guilty just for thinking we've let someone down. Here's the thing, though; guilt is toxic. It's not a productive emotion. When we're busy beating ourselves up by feeling guilty, we're losing a tremendous amount of energy and motivation. Guilt causes an enormous emotional and intellectual drain. Most of the time we don't take action to stop it or correct the situation. We just keep beating ourselves up and feel worse and worse."

"You nailed that!" Alex shook his head. "So what can I do?"

"Stop feeling guilty," Mike said. "I know, I know. Easier said than done. But 99% of the things we fear never come true. We suffer by imagining what could happen, rather than dealing with what is happening. Fear leads to worry, and worry without control over something is very counter-productive."

"And exhausting," Alex said. "I'm tired all the time. I am tired of fighting, I am tired of protecting, I am tired of explaining, I just want to stop, I can't sleep, I can't focus, I feel like I am always running away. I keep asking myself, will it ever end? When I'm at home, I can't rest; when I'm at work I cannot concentrate. Fear is affecting both my personal life and my professional life, and I don't know how to stop it."

Optimism

"Welcome to being a man," Mike said. "You are not the first, and you won't be the last to feel that way. From early childhood, boys are conditioned and taught to fight and conquer their fears, to overcome them if they want to be a 'real man.' We're never told to embrace our fears, or to look for lessons and learn from our fears. I'm guessing Adam is struggling with this right now, too.

"Society rewards us for compartmentalizing our emotions and isolating ourselves when we feel these negative emotions, right?"

"Yes," Alex said. He frowned, thinking about what Mike had just said and wondering where he might be going with the concept of fear.

"Is there a different way to deal with it?"

"Yes, and no. You see, we mentally and emotionally isolate ourselves from our fears. This feeling of being socially and emotionally isolated and alone actually makes us more miserable. You know, research has shown this feeling of isolation can increase chances of early death by 14%. Even the Dalai Lama lamented the feeling of being isolated, not because of being alone, but the feeling of being someone different, which he actually is, created a fear of separation and loneliness.

"Nelson Mandela admitted that there were days in the prison when they were afraid no one would make it out alive. He later said, 'I learned that courage was not the absence of fear, but the triumph over it. The brave man is not he who does not feel afraid, but he who conquers that fear.'"

"That's most of the men I know," Alex said. "I think that's just our lot in life."

"Well, if you think it is then you're most likely to live that viewpoint," Mike said. "But let me tell you about a man named Viktor Frankl, a Jewish psychiatrist who was imprisoned in the death camps of Nazi Germany. He was among many men, but also very isolated in the middle of a large community, all of whom were just as terrified, fearful, mistrustful and alone as he was.

"He went through torture, indignation, and pain, and lived under constant fear of being killed at any time by being sent to the gas chambers. One day while lying naked and alone in a small room, he discovered that he could overcome fear through the same imagination based on the fundamental principle of embryonic freedom – it's the nature of man that *between stimulus and response, he has the freedom to choose.*

"His awareness wasn't just a thought. It was science. Stress, anxiety, and sleeplessness are all manifestations of fear. In fact, our stress response is our defense mechanism against fear. When we experience fear, cortisol and adrenalin are released into our bloodstream. That causes our pupils to dilate so that we can see better. It speeds up our breathing and reflexes so we respond quicker. Our blood is directed to our larger muscles so that we can fight or run faster. These changes in our physical state actually helped our ancestors survive while facing huge beasts that were perhaps ten times their size."

"But we're not fighting lions, tigers, and and bears now," Alex said.

"True, but our bodies haven't changed even though our environments have. Fear still makes us alert, agile, and ready, which may be good when you need that kind of response. Being in a state of constant stress, response without a natural release of that stress will lead to fatigue, depression, illness and even aging."

"So, short of running a mile every time I feel stressed, what can I do?" Alex asked.

"Develop *stress resilience or stoicism.* You are a businessman, right? There's been a lot of recent research in neuroscience regarding stress. I was just reading a study published on something called 'productive paranoia.' This suggests that successful entrepreneurs who practiced productive paranoia, which is just the ability to be hyper-vigilant about potentially bad events that can hit your company, did better than those who didn't.

"Instead of dismissing the fears or fighting them, they were able to turn their fears into preparation and clearheaded action. They read up on what scared them, defined and studied the actual fear they were having, and then they translated that fear into preparation and action. So that way, if their worst fears were to come true, their businesses were ready to respond."

"That's interesting," Alex said. He could sense the excitement in his tone, as could Mike.

"Ah, you like that," Mike said.

Optimism

"Yes. It makes me feel less helpless. You're telling me that there is something I can do about my fear rather than just stew in it. I feel more empowered, like I have control over my fear. I can do something more than meditate or think about it. I can take action!"

Mike nodded. "You can. You know, fear responses have been a subject of study for probably as long as fear has existed. However, instead of the compartmentalized response I was explaining earlier, we need to have a comprehensive response. So with any form of fear response, be it in Viktor Frankl's *ability to choose* response, building *stress resilience, stoicism,* or practicing *productive paranoia,* there has to be a deep and profound sense of gratitude. Therefore, the best reaction to fear would be to develop an attitude of gratitude. I know it doesn't sound like a viable way to eliminate fear, but it is. You don't have to be a strong person, or a talented or especially capable manager or CEO. You just have to be grateful.

"Gratitude is the truest form of defense. I know that sounds odd, but gratitude can help us truly like ourselves by accepting *who* we are and *what* we have. Accept as fact that you are one among many, that you are not special and don't need to struggle to prove that you are special, that you don't have to put yourself on a lofty pedestal. You may not be special but you are *unique*. We all are. We are all an absolutely unique soul, and we need to be that way – the way we were at birth when we didn't care about what people around us were saying about us.

"It is a fear of not having enough, of scarcity, or the fear of rejection, or the fear of not being special that has brought us all a whole lot of negativity, anxiety, and stress in life. Most people undervalue what they have and overvalue what they don't. But when we have gratitude for who we are and what we have, we develop a sense of being better than many of the seven-and-a-half billion people in the world, and in fact, absolutely *unique*. Gratitude can take us from feeling sorry for ourselves to feeling comfortable with ourselves.

"Neuroscientists have shown that we as human beings are hardwired optimists, and gratitude is the birthplace of Optimism. Gratitude frees us from emotional pain. So if you want to let go of emotional pain, choose gratitude.

"Gratitude is especially powerful at healing childhood wounds, the deep scars of shame and guilt, the sense of victimhood that you have been carrying rooted in feelings of helplessness, limiting beliefs, isolation, and disenchantment.

"What's important, Alex, is for you to take charge. By that, I mean take total ownership and make yourself the center of your experience. You have to believe that you can control your life and manage things. Stop the vampires from haunting you with the negative commentary. Stop judging yourself in terms of who you are, how you look, what happened to you, or what you did or didn't do. You are no saint.

You are no messiah. You are not perfect. We all have our share of flaws. We all make our share of mistakes. You don't need to pretend to be perfect. You do have to say, 'Here I am as I am. I am thankful for where I am and who I am, and if I am thankful, then you have to accept me the way I am.'"

"I can do that," Alex said. "But I really don't see that it's going to make a difference. It seems too simple."

"It's the simplest things that are the most powerful. Levers, oil on gears, the wheel. Something doesn't have to be complex to work, and work well. Don't judge things by how complex or complicated they are. True genius is in simplicity.

"Be thankful for who you are, for what you have, and what you have achieved. Genuine gratitude replaces victimhood with joy. There is no more self pity when there is an infinite supply of things to be grateful for. Think about others whose plights are perhaps worse than yours. They survive or even thrive. Why? How?

Being grateful gives us a sense of fulfillment, a sense of *enough* and that leads to embracing fear. Because while you have this manifestation of fear, you also have the reality that you are a successful businessman. You have a stable income. You have single-handedly given Adam all the comforts of life. He has turned out to be a smart, good-looking lad. Together you have come a long way and have a lot to be thankful for."

Alex suddenly sat up straighter as he intently listened to Mike. Mike was right. He could feel it in his gut. He didn't even need to reason it out. A sense of pride overtook his fears. The melancholy and misery that had engulfed him only minutes before suddenly seemed to transform into positivity and gratitude. He could feel a secure sense of emotional courage, a comforting feeling of self-acceptance, of worthiness and renewed energy. Alex remembered something he had learned in school. Thornton Wilder had once said, "We can only be said to be alive in those moments when our hearts are conscious of our treasures."

Alex felt his fears transform into a kind of positive energy, and he reflected upon his successful business career. He took in a deep breath and exhaled. He could feel a tingle as Mike spoke.

"So back to Becky's story," Mike exclaimed. "You are absolutely right. She practiced gratitude for what she *did* have, not anger or resentment for what she lacked. Think about how easy it would have been for her to grumble about the unfairness of it all. Hell, there are *still* times when I gripe about certain things not going my way, and look at what I have!" He gestured to the huge mansion behind them, and the patio, pool, and gardens before them.

"I am definitely guilty of that, too," Alex said, staring down at his hands. He didn't want to lose this feeling he was having, like he was somehow lit from the inside.

He thought about all of the times he had resented others for small mishaps in his life, or his growing bitterness over the situation with his son Adam. Really, he should be grateful for riches in his life! He had two healthy, smart, active sons, an amazing and supportive wife, a fulfilling job at a successful company, and so much more. Why had he chosen to focus on only the negative?

"Becky's situation may seem very dire to you and me," continued Mike. "But she chose gratitude over bellyaching. She made a choice. That's why gratitude is the place from where all optimism stems. If you are thankful, you have a sense of abundance. You're always open to being optimistic. Even God says, in essence, 'If you are thankful, I will give you more.' Once you have this attitude of gratitude, it gives you confidence. You see, Alex, it all begins with consciousness. You can either choose to be grateful by developing a consciousness around what you have and focusing on it, or you can choose to be ungrateful by focusing on things that you do not have.

"Another unexpected benefit of gratitude is that it helps you establish better social connections."

"Wait," said Alex. "I get that gratitude can give you confidence, and I see how that, in turn, gives you emotional courage. But how does it help you to establish better social connections?"

Mike laughed. "Great question! I was hoping you'd pick up on the jump there. The piece you're missing is the understanding that gratitude not only helps you see the good in you and your own life, it also helps you see the good in others. Think about it like this: our companies are often identified by their leaders. I'm sure many people think of you when they think of your company. I know I'm often recognized as the *face* of my company, even though I haven't worked there in any official capacity in years!

"But our companies could never, ever run without the dozens, hundreds, or in my case, thousands of employees who put in hours of hard work, day in and day out. I'm talking about every single employee: the janitors, the mail room employees, the programmers, the machinists, everybody. You lose one person, and there's an immediate imbalance. Others have to pick up the slack. So be grateful for these people and the value they *all* bring. Look for the gold in people, not the dirt. When you find one nugget, you'll look for more. It's self-perpetuating.

"Gratitude brings about an air of positivity. It creates a sense of grace in you. You tend to be happier, cheerful, and more gregarious. Who wouldn't want to be around a person who's fun and attractive? When this happens, people automatically flock to you. Gratitude positively impacts our mental states, making us happier, more social, more trusting, and more receptive to interaction with others.

"Try saying 'thank you' with a frown on your face. When you genuinely thank someone with your whole heart, you will invariably smile, and when you smile, there will be miles of that smile. Then the law of attraction kicks in. People will be attracted to that smiling, happy face. It's a face that will get you

Optimism

socially connected, even to strangers. You'll create an aura of positivity. That will make everything work in your favor."

Alex laughed and rolled his eyes.

"Ah, but there's science to prove this," Mike said. "Positivity releases dopamine in your bloodstream that makes you happier and also opens you up for learning new things. Trust me here. You'll start seeing every social interaction as a new learning experience."

"If you say so," Alex said.

Mike smiled, and continued. "Let me tell you an interesting episode. I was a board member of a pharmaceutical company in the UK. I was invited to their strategy retreat, a two-day event. The meeting was started by a consulting company giving a very thorough presentation on the world's economy, Europe's economy, and the UK's economy before moving onto the pharmaceutical industry. They highlighted trends and identified opportunities and challenges in the industry.

"This was followed by a hilarious skit presented by the employees of the company that left the attendees enthralled. Actually, that was the theme throughout the event. Every serious business discussion was followed by something hilarious and fun. A senior executive later told me that this was very carefully planned under the supervision of the CEO himself. It was this positive leadership that kept the entire organization engaged and cohesive. Even at work, every day there would be some surprise for the employees that would keep them happy, positive, laughing, and engaged."

Alex nodded. "Interesting."

Mike continued, "Optimism comes to life when you start seeing good in people."

"So it's about recognizing people's talents and strengths, rather than dwelling on their shortcomings?" Alex asked.

"Yes, in a way. You still want to encourage excellence in everyone. I'll have much more to say about excellence later, but acknowledging people's good qualities, their talents, and their efforts in life is paramount. That doesn't mean you ignore their failures and shortcomings. You want to address those with feedback and even discipline where it's needed, but mostly you want to focus on what people are doing right.

"I read a book called *The Failure-Tolerant Leader* years ago. I probably still have it in my library. The author argued that when you start seeing the good in people, you'll begin to foster a work environment where successes and setbacks are both treated as learning experiences. There has been some incredible work done in this area, for instance, Martin Seligman's work on *Building Resilience* and Carol Dweck's work on *Growth Mindset*.

But I believe the key to seeing good in people is being able to recognize our intrinsic biases first."

"Hmmm," Alex said, "I've heard about bias but not about *intrinsic* and *extrinsic* bias."

"Good catch, Alex. Let me explain. Intrinsic biases are subconscious stereotypes that affect the way we make decisions. They come from societal cues we've been exposed to our entire lives. They get entrenched in our subconscious, and for the most part, we're completely unaware of them. However, they have a profound impact on the way we function. They affect the way employers subconsciously select between potential candidates, the way we interact with people, and even the way we make friends."

"I can see that. We're a product of our upbringing, environment, and family. At least to a degree," Alex said.

"Exactly, only most of us don't realize that. Let me tell you an interesting case we experienced at one of my companies. We were interviewing candidates for a very senior position, a vice president post. The process was a very elaborate one. The company was overly meticulous about it, even hiring an external consultant for the whole thing. Anyway, we got to the final stage, a panel interview for the six candidates that made it to our short list. I was one of the panel members.

"We met with each candidate for almost three hours. It was pretty hectic. We had agreed that the candidate had to be a consensus candidate and that all the panel members must agree on one candidate. Finally, we were getting close to zeroing in on one candidate, but one panel member did not agree with us. So we asked him what he had against the candidate, and he gave us a few good reasons. So we decided to invite the candidate back for another round of interviews.

"What we really wanted to do was probe deeper into the areas where the one panel member had expressed doubts. The interview went very well, and we were all even more convinced that this was the candidate we wanted.

"But this same panel member said he needed more time to think because he still wasn't sure. We were very surprised but left it at that and decided to give him some time to think. Later, one of the other panel members met up with this member to have a one-on-one chat with him, and it turned out that his first wife had attended the same college as this candidate. She was very proud of being an alumna; so much so, that it had led to their divorce. So this panel member had developed an intrinsic bias that people from this college had an air of arrogance and hot-headedness. It was his bias, not any fact or true characteristic of this candidate, that had him hesitating on hiring him."

"That is really interesting," Alex said, trying to think of a time when he had done something similar. I almost didn't ask my second wife out on our first date because when we met she was wearing an outfit similar to one that my first wife used to wear. I thought it was a sign," he laughed. "I never really thought about it, but now that you mention it, I can see how intrinsic bias can affect us in ways we don't even realize."

"Yes, so embracing diversity in all its forms is one way to see the good in everyone. Discriminating on the basis of position, socioeconomic status, skin color, gender, or age is a good way to shut down optimism completely. Remember, Wangari Maathai saw the good, the potential, in the women from her own country, and her belief in their talents and hard work led to a global movement for change.

"She demonstrated tremendous resilience. She faced setbacks. She was arrested and beaten, but she came back so much stronger and determined every time life knocked her down. She stood strong in the face of adversity. Her resilience was the result of accepting the reality that fighting an establishment that didn't care much about women and their rights was not going to be easy.

"But the movement she launched was deep-rooted in her core values, and she was absolutely pragmatic about making changes. She improvised where she had to, and when she launched the Green Belt Movement, she said, "I will be a hummingbird; I will do the best I can.""

"She sure inspired others to make positive changes," Alex said.

"Yes, she did. She also established unique connections and embraced diversity by rallying women from diverse backgrounds. Those women brought their own different perspectives. They were able to see situations, problems, solutions, and processes from different angles, then leverage new connections and establish new bonds to usher in a new era," Mike said.

"And she did it all simply by fostering a culture of positivity wherever she went. Imagine walking into a small village in Kenya and telling the women there that they can create jobs for their community, reduce poverty, improve environmental conditions, and hold leaders accountable. All by planting a tree. Can you imagine? How do you keep the momentum going from one small action?"

"You hope others will stay positive with you?" asked Alex.

"You *force* positivity into every situation and every culture," corrected Mike. "By force, I don't mean you use physical, emotional, or mental intimidation. Rather, you do by *showing*. Make adversity look small by starting with the little things: changes in language and conversation, smiling, lifting people up rather than tearing them down. Tackle big problems by breaking them down into smaller components. Don't ever give in to the impulse to unfairly criticize, beat down, or belittle another human being.

"Pretty soon, those small changes will add up to a whole culture of positivity that shines through in everything you do. And those you've helped will themselves become ambassadors of positivity in everything *they* do. It's a ripple effect. It's achieved by you making it happen. Not waiting until it happens to you."

"I see," Alex said. "So I need to have an attitude of possibility instead of *im*possibility."

Optimism

"Yes!" Mike said, raising his hands in the air. "I think you're really getting it now. In addition to positivity, you need to have a can-do attitude about everything you set out to accomplish. When you put a positive veneer around yourself, as we just discussed, you will attract your true friends and those who can work well with you. It will allow you to set and then accomplish long-term goals.

"Give up immediate pleasures to reach for those bigger goals. Finally, you will find in yourself that confidence which stems from action. Do you see how all of these tenets work toward building confidence in you and confidence in others? True confidence is so important, and it helps you convey your true, authentic self to others as well. And we know how important authenticity is!" Mike laughed.

Alex chuckled. "We sure do! I'm beginning to see it even more now. Honestly, sometimes I forget that positivity and *can-do* are even options."

"That's totally understandable," reassured Mike. "It happens to all of us, especially in the business world, because we're often conditioned to think of worst-case scenarios and to be vigilant against waste in the workplace. These situations can promote *re*activity rather than *pro*activity.

"I want you to repeat this phrase to yourself every day, whenever you find yourself at a loss or in a particularly negative mindset: 'I can do.' You try it."

"I can do this," Alex said.

"Say it again," Mike said. "In fact, say it five times in a row. And each time, I want you to say it with more gusto."

"Okay," Alex laughed. He knew Mike was serious, but it seemed like such a silly thing to say out loud. Was this really necessary? The feeling of lightness he'd just experienced was beginning to fade. That had been unexpected, but Mike had been right about gratitude. He was probably right about this. He wanted to learn from Mike, and it was clear setting aside his disbeliefs came with the territory. He sat up a little higher and began.

"I can do this. I can do ... this."

"Louder," Mike said. "Don't drone. Put your passion into it. Do you really believe you can do it? I'm not so sure hearing you now."

"I can do this," Alex raised his voice and thought about Mike's lessons on positivity and courage. He *could* do this. "I can do this. I CAN DO THIS!" he finished the last statement with a shout that echoed through the spacious patio area.

"Good!" Mike beamed with what Alex assumed was pride. "It's a great start. What I've just gotten you to do is *imagine* the possibility for something better. Always try to make your 'I Can' stronger than your IQ.' This brings me to the fifth and final tenet for optimism: Imagination and Creativity.

"Albert Einstein – one of the greatest minds to ever live. I love his quotes. Let me find my favorite." Mike riffled through the pages until he landed on one in the middle. "Aha! Here it is: Imagination is more important than knowledge. For knowledge is limited, whereas imagination embraces the entire world, stimulating progress, giving birth to evolution."

"Oh yeah," Alex said, tapping his finger to his lips. "I think I remember hearing that first part somewhere."

"Likely, it was at an innovation training or in a book on innovation. Those guys put a lot of emphasis on imagination," replied Mike. "And for good reason! Imagination helps stimulate the parts of you that prize activity, possibility, and fearlessness. Tapping into your imagination allows you to think of all that's possible for you and for your organization. Then, you have to get creative with how you use your imagination to solve problems. Creativity and imagination are absolutely essential skills in business and in life. I don't think enough people realize just how important they are."

"I think a lot of people are afraid to put value in them," Alex said. "In many of the meetings and conferences I attend, these are seen as *soft* skills or characteristics, and are often not teachable. Those who can use creativity and imagination well are seen as being *gifted* with them. In fact…" Alex hesitated.

Mike laughed. "You think it's an inherent condition as well?"

"Well, yeah, kind of," Alex shrugged. "I'm not a very creative person, and I sometimes have trouble imagining different ways a project or situation could go. But others seem to be very good at it, so I figure they're just born with it, you know?"

Optimism

"Could be," Mike said. "Or, it could be that they took the time, energy, and *courage* to explore their imagination and creativity and practiced how it might help them solve business problems. Over time, they became so good at it that it seemed like second nature."

"Back to courage," Alex laughed.

"Absolutely! In order to develop these skills, those people had to take ownership, tap into their strengths and express their desires to learn these skills. And they had to maintain positivity and optimism while they did so. Courage is an essential part of optimism, and being optimistic helps you find the emotional courage. They feed one another.

"In fact, I'm going to let you in on a little secret. All five of these pillars enhance and support one another. You've only learned about two so far, but you can already see how deeply they're intertwined. They're like the ingredients of a really excellent pasta sauce. Each contributes their own unique flavor to the sauce, but the sauce itself would not exist, in all its greatness, without all the ingredients."

"That's true," said Alex slowly, thinking about his great-grandmother's famous pesto sauce. "You lose just one component, and it's a completely different tasting experience."

"You got it!" Mike smiled, "It's called a gestalt, where the organized whole is perceived as more than the sum of its parts." He raised his glass in a toast. Alex did the same. They clinked their glasses and took a sip.

"Now," said Mike, once he finished, "I've got an assignment for you."

"More reading?" inquired Alex.

"Nope," said Mike. "Like the last one, this one's a little more practical.

Next time you go into the office, I want you to practice these two tenets. You can do that however you see fit. I'll leave it up to you. But I want you to take your son Adam with you when you do."

"Adam?" worried Alex. He'd been dutifully listening to Mike these past few months, reading and practicing what he'd learned in small doses. But to bring these new ideas to the office so soon, and with his son in tow? He wasn't even sure how he'd get Adam to accompany him. Come to think of it, Alex couldn't remember the last time he'd even invited Adam or David to visit him at work.

Mike noticed his hesitation and smiled. "I know this may seem like a tough assignment, Alex, but I have no doubt you can handle it. Remember what Winston Churchill said: Success is not final, failure is not fatal: it is the courage to continue that counts."

Alex sighed halfheartedly. "I suppose that's why courage is the first pillar you talk about."

"It's first for many reasons." Mike was silent for a moment, studying Alex's face, looking for a response. "Remember, drop your fear of being exposed. That will help make you confident. Don't let your confidence get submerged under all kinds of negative beliefs." Mike stood and offered his hand to Alex.

"Best of luck. But you don't need luck. You can do this. One parting piece of advice that I also give myself: Don't let that innate confidence you were born with get diminished. Go get 'em. I look forward to hearing the results next time we meet."

IN SUMMARY:

Optimism is the belief that if something has to happen it will happen, and if it doesn't, then something better will happen.

The five tenets of Optimism are:

- **Gratitude.** Gratitude is an attitude of appreciation for what we have, emotionally, spiritually, physically, and economically, rather than what we want or wish for. Gratitude is positive psychology. Studies show that we can deliberately cultivate gratitude to develop the emotional courage that can help us improve our well-being and happiness. In fact an attitude of gratitude is associated with increased energy, a sense of abundance, empathy and social relations, and spiritual connectedness to the universe.

Optimism

- **Can-do attitude.** A can-do attitude is a positive attitude about your ability to achieve success – an aura of confidence. It's about believing you *can* rather than you *can't*. People with can-do attitudes are willing, excited, and hopeful about tackling new tasks, even those that they dislike or find difficult. An uncanny ability to put a positive veneer to any situation. A can-do attitude helps you identify your true friends and see through the nay sayers, the energy drainers. The good news is if you don't have the confidence to do this, you can develop it.
- **See the good in people.** By the time we become adults we have learned to form quick assessments about people. By the time we're in our 40s and 50s, our habits about how we form opinions about others are entrenched, especially in the workplace. But consciously seeing good in people and valuing them for *who* they are will make us more socially resilient and emotionally intelligent, and it will also enhance our self-worth. By embracing diversity, we begin to value humanity. People are often only different because of their different experiences.

    It is said everything that irritates us about others helps us understand ourselves better. Developing a healthy sense of self and genuine concern for others offers freedom from hostility and fear. Giving someone the benefit of the doubt and deliberately looking for the positive judgment, rather than the negative one, guarantees we'll be closer to the actual truth. Elisabeth Kubler Ross once said, "We often criticize the things in other people that we fear most in ourselves."
- **Creativity and innovation.** Albert Einstein said, "Imagination is more important than knowledge." Imagination is the basis of creativity and innovation that breeds optimism. Creativity refers to generating new and unique ideas. It helps you become fearless, overcome the feeling of shame, and try new things. Creativity is about *unleashing the potential* of the mind to conceive new ideas and challenge assumptions. It helps you become wiser and more adaptable.
- **Force Positivity.** Life is a journey where we experience euphoric highs and demoralizing lows. The one common goal we all seek is happiness.

But happiness does not depend upon *who we are* and *what we have*. It depends on *how we think* and *what we do for others*. Happiness increases or decreases due to gaps between our expectations and our mostly subjective reality.

The secret to long-lasting happiness, however, is to see life as a journey where a little sorrow is as much a part of the journey as is a little sunshine. This sorrow or sunshine can be extended by making adversity seem small and bringing hope to the hopeless. You can develop the tenacity to break through the borders of affliction and make every adversity small by lifting up and giving support and hope to those who are down trodden. Oprah Winfrey expressed it well when she said, "What you focus on expands, and when you focus on the goodness in your life, you create more of it."

Chapter Five

THE OFFICE VISIT

Alex sighed as he looked through his talking points for the strategy session tomorrow. He was more nervous about the session than he cared to admit to anyone. Unfortunately, the company's quarterly projections had taken a dive, and Alex had the tough task of explaining what went wrong to his investors. He was hoping to introduce a few new programs that would help right the ship, and use Mike's teachings around courage and optimism to sell them. He actually wished he had a year with nothing more to do than focus on Mike's teaching. But maybe this was the sort of thing Mike considered hands-on. He sighed deeply and leaned back in his office chair, frowning at the papers, reports, and print out of his slide presentation.

He'd hoped to invite Adam to something inspiring, something that made him look capable, not weak. This wasn't the sort of recruiting image that won converts.

Alex had hoped Adam's presence at the meeting would help him learn more about the business and hopefully spark his interest in working for him. Who'd want to work for a loser though? He stopped himself. Negative self talk. "I CAN DO THIS," he said out loud.

Adam had just finished the school year and hadn't yet started his summer job as a lifeguard, so he had time to accompany Alex to the early morning meeting. He could meet a lot of key people at the company and start getting his feet wet in the family business before college, which would greatly help his admission chances and give him a career goal for school to boot.

Alex loathed that his son had rejected his offer to work for him this summer, but he knew he couldn't force the issue. Instead, he hoped to show him what a steady path through the family business could bring him: a great career as an important and well-respected businessman. It would be hard to compete with girls, sunshine and a swimming pool, and all the adolescent glory of being a lifeguard, but he would try.

The problem was Alex hadn't quite found the right time to ask him along yet. He peered over his shoulder. Adam was sitting at the family dining table, absorbed in whatever was happening on his iPhone. Alex figured this was as good a time as any, and he took a deep breath.

"Son," he exclaimed, walking over to Adam and thumping him hard on the back. "I have a great idea. I've got to lead a company meeting tomorrow, and I think you'd get a kick out of seeing your old man front and center. Why don't you come with me? It'll get you out of the house, and we can go out to lunch after. Just you and me! What do you say?" He pasted a grin on his face.

Adam briefly glanced at Alex before returning to his phone. "I don't think so, Dad. That doesn't sound like much fun."

"Oh, it'll be great!" Alex urged. "You can learn all about the business, and it'll get you out of the house for a little while. Maybe you'll even put the phone down for five minutes," he joked.

Adam sighed and turned to look at his father. "I'm not just messing around on my phone, Dad. I'm looking at a Kickstarter project for a drone that my friend Kyle is building. If he gets funded, I'll help him write the Java API code to program it."

Alex blinked, confused by the conversation. What was Kickstarter and Java API? He was not a tech person, although his son had tried to teach him the basic terminology around coding. But that was, what, four years ago? Alex couldn't remember.

"Oh, okay," Alex replied weakly. "Well, the meeting tomorrow—"

"Adam, honey, you should go with your dad," Beverly, Alex's wife, called out as she breezed in from the kitchen. "I know you've got your coding camp next week and you want a little down time, but this would be a good opportunity to

The Office Visit

talk with a few folks who could give you some advice on your new algorithm. He can meet a few of your tech people, right, Al?" she asked as she placed a bowl of fresh fruit on the table and sat down beside her son.

Alex felt even more confused. Coding camp? Algorithm? He couldn't remember Adam or Bev telling him anything about this. "Uh, sure," he replied distractedly.

Adam stood up. "Fine. As long as that's part of the deal." He turned and left for his room, still scrolling through his phone.

Alex plopped down in Adam's recently-vacated seat and heaved a long sigh. "I had no idea he was so interested in programming and all this computer stuff. And drones? Did you tell me he was doing coding camp?"

"Yes, Al, I did," Beverly chided, plucking an apple from the fruit bowl. "I mentioned it to you three weeks ago, and again last week after my client dinner. Did you not listen to me?"

"I listened," snapped Alex. "I just had a lot going on that week. The acquisition plans for that plant in Carlyle had just fallen through, and I had to prep for the big budget meeting with the finance and development committees."

"You always have big meetings, and plans, and crises, Alex," Beverly reminded him. "And they always take your attention away from your family. Adam especially. When was the last time you did something with him?"

"That's what I'm trying to do now!" Alex cried.

"Let me finish. When was the last time you did something with him not revolving around your business? You've been pushing him for months to learn more about the company and work there over the summer, but he's just not interested. Let him take his own path, like I did."

Alex mentally cursed. He and his second wife had been down this path many, many times. Bev had a flair for creativity and a sharp independent streak, two of the qualities that had attracted him to her in the first place. These qualities had led her to start her own small graphic design firm several years ago, not long after they had married and Bev had had Adam. Bev loved the freedom of being her own boss and frequently mentioned this to her husband and sons.

"I wish she also mentioned all the difficulties involved and the discipline required for starting a business too," thought Alex grumpily.

While Bev was clearly talented and fully capable of running her own firm, in Alex's opinion she didn't have the greatest business sense. She often underestimated the dedication needed to build her business and book clients. She and her team only engaged two or three accounts a year. In Alex's opinion, that number should be in the double digits. Alex often thought that if she just applied herself and paid more attention to the market and potential growth areas, she could build a truly successful business worth millions. But Bev seemed more interested in boasting to her friends about her independent lifestyle and her client relationships than growing her company (all while, of course, enjoying the financial perks of Alex's hard work). Alex was fearful that Bev would pass this cavalier, arrogant attitude on to Adam. He had told her as much many times, and that conversation always ended the same: with Bev storming off in a huff. Alex couldn't say this time would be any different.

"But Bev, if he doesn't apply himself, he'll fall behind and lack the discipline to make the right career choices," argued Alex. "If he's interested in coding and all that, he'll be entering a really competitive field. He needs some business sense to stay ahead of the curve."

"And he can get that in college," Bev countered. "I know you want him to follow in your footsteps, Al, but he's a creative independent like me. He'd probably learn more from shadowing me than you right now, to be honest."

"Let's not do this, Bev," sighed Alex. "You know I think your business is great, but Adam needs more discipline in his life."

"Discipline I can't provide. I get it," sniffed Beverly. "You know, you should tell your friend Mike to teach you some humility and tact to go along with your *courage* and *optimism*." Her last words dripped with sarcasm. She stood up.

"Bev, don't leave," Alex reached for her, but she shrugged his hand off her wrist. She walked towards the kitchen and turned to face Alex when she reached the doorway.

The Office Visit

"Al, a word of advice. Let Adam make up his own mind about his future. You may think you know what's best for him, but you can't force him to do what you want. He's got to want it, too. You just have to trust him, or you run the risk of losing him." Beverly disappeared into the kitchen.

Alex sat back and thought about Bev's comment. *You just have to trust him, or you run the risk of losing him.* His mind turned to Mike and all the ideas about authenticity, courage, and optimism he had learned over the past few months. They made sense when he read them and when Mike explained them. But try as he might, he just couldn't see how he could apply them to his situation with Adam. How was he supposed to get vulnerable with Adam when he couldn't get the kid to stay in the same room with him? How could he be optimistic and force positivity around Bev, who left conversations when they got a little tough? It had all seemed so much easier in Mike's presence.

He hoped tomorrow would go better. It just had to. Shaking his head, Alex pulled out his talking points for the meeting and began reviewing them once again.

***

Alex stepped out of his Lexus and pulled on his crisp suit jacket. Today was the big strategy meeting, and he was both excited and nervous to apply what he'd learned from Mike to make some real changes within his company. Adam had agreed to come with him, although reluctantly.

He hoped Adam would truly listen and try to understand why he wanted him to be a part of the company. He saw real potential in Adam to be a key part of his business. Of the family business, he corrected himself. Adam just needed to see Alex at work with his new knowledge, and he would get it.

Speaking of – he glanced over to the passenger door as Adam emerged, his plain black suit already rumpled from the brief car ride. Alex frowned and walked over to Adam.

"You should have taken your jacket off for the car ride," Alex chided as he straightened his son's tie and smoothed his shoulders. Adam shrugged away from his father and crossed his arms across his chest. "Dad, it's fine," he mumbled.

Alex sighed. He knew he was nitpicking Adam, but he couldn't help it. Maybe now was the time to try a little of that optimism and force positivity to boost Adam's spirits. He turned and looked at the clear blue sky.

"Boy, it's a great day today, isn't it?" Alex boomed. "Let's be thankful for this beautiful sky and remember all that we have to offer. We're going to make some great strides today!" He turned and beamed at Adam.

Adam peered up at the sky from behind his sunglasses. "I guess," he mumbled.

"We will! Now, I've got a detailed agenda for you here." Alex passed Adam a small binder with the company logo emblazoned on the cover. "It's got some paper in there for you to take notes. I can have my assistant Carla get you a pen if you didn't bring one. I'd like for you to think about some of the programs and ideas I'm going to propose today and what you might like to take on as a long-term project. We could probably get you in on a planning session with the marketing department next—"

"Dad!" cried Adam. "Just slow down! I said I'd come to the meeting, but that's all! I already told you like a million times, I've got other plans for college and stuff. You can't just expect me to do whatever you say. I'm not earning money for chores or whatever here." He stomped off to the building entrance.

Alex shook his head. His son still didn't get it. All he could do now was hope for the best and lead a great strategy meeting today. He followed Adam into the building, trying desperately to maintain his optimism and boost his courage for the session ahead.

***

"So, as you can see, our quarterly projections are a bit lower than we had initially thought," Alex addressed the company investors, strategy specialists, and executives assembled in the large conference room. "While this obviously isn't great, I've drafted a few proposals and come up with some innovative ideas

The Office Visit

that will help us get this company back on track." Alex nodded at Carla, who began handing out binders to the assembled group.

She smiled sympathetically when she reached Adam, who waved the binder Alex had given him earlier and gave her a warm smile. The poor kid looked bored out of his mind, stuck inside at a board meeting of all places on such a nice day. "What is Alex thinking?" she mused. "What could the kid really learn at an hours-long strategy session?" Alex had shared with her some of his hopes around employing Adam and grooming him to eventually lead the business, but Carla privately thought her boss was pushing his son way too hard down a path he clearly didn't want to go.

Besides, allowing a teenager into a meeting with sensitive company information seemed, well, ill-advised at best. She had already seen a few executives glancing at Adam during the meeting. Alex's introduction of his son had raised a few eyebrows, mainly because Alex had spent ten minutes sharing way too much about his son's need to focus on the business and ordering others to give him access to company accounts and sensitive information. Adam was a great kid, no doubt, but the personal details discussed and requested seemed excessive.

"If you'll turn to the first page," Alex was saying to the group, "you can see a plan I've laid out for a new strategic initiative I'm calling 'Innovation In Line.' I think it'll really help us streamline our manufacturing assembly lines and improve the services we offer by tapping into our creativity and courage. You know, we have a great wealth of talent throughout our company, but I think we can use it in better and more innovative ways."

Alex pulled up a powerpoint slide with a crowded-looking illustration in the middle. At the top, a bright red thought bubble shouted the words 'Innovation in Line!' The diagram showed a variety of people in silhouette, each with their own thought bubbles describing a small project they had created and would champion in their workplaces. Each idea was connected by a line. On the right side of the page, that line turned into an arrow that pushed against a circle labeled 'Status Quo.' The arrow's point of impact against the circle was labeled 'Disruption.'

"The folks in this picture represent our manufacturing workers," Alex said. "They are the front lines in our implementation of innovation and creativity. We want to tap into their enthusiasm and give them projects that can help them establish a better workplace for themselves, a more positive and caring culture that promotes a can-do attitude of energy, optimism, and ownership." He clicked to the next slide, this one depicting one of the silhouetted workers and their innovation idea in full. "You can see here that these workers' project is to redesign their work station so they can more quickly move through their portion of the manufacturing process. It also has the added benefit of improving their comfort while they work, leading to a happier, more productive working environment."

Alex looked out into the crowd. No one seemed particularly moved by his great idea. In fact, several skeptical faces scrutinized his slide and the binders in front of them. Alex pressed on.

"These kinds of ideas can really change an organization from the ground up. We want everyone to feel involved in the company culture. We want them to feel empowered by their work, courageous and wholly themselves as they pursue excellence. 'Innovation in Line' is designed to help them find this courage to be themselves and exercise their creativity."

"But they're not picking these projects out for themselves, are they, Alex?" inquired Henry, Alex's VP of Business Development.

"Well, no," admitted Alex. "There are still very specific things we want them to accomplish through these projects, so the ideas are coming from upstairs, so to speak. But they will be given full ownership over how to manage and execute them."

"Where are they supposed to find the time for this?" asked the COO, Carolina. "I mean, I see what you're going for here, Alex, but this seems like a lot of additional work for a workforce that's already incredibly pressured for results. Are they going to work on these little projects during their regular shifts?"

"And how are we going to fund them?" interjected another voice from the back of the room. Alex could tell this was Marlene, his Chief Financial Officer.

The Office Visit

"Some of those ideas on the previous slide seem relatively expensive with little ROI. What's our plan for the finances?"

"Okay," Alex waved his hands. "I know there are some questions about all of this, but if you could just wait—"

"Who's going to oversee all of this and make sure they stay on track?" someone else asked.

"Are we expected to have projects as well?" asked another executive. More murmurs arose from the group.

It was clear to Alex that he had lost them. He had anticipated a few of these questions – namely the budget and management ones – but he hadn't thought there would be objections to doing this on regular company time. He was also taken aback by the first question from Henry. Should he have changed the format to allow employees their choice in projects? When he was creating this, he thought that management and the higher-ups would know best. But now he wasn't so sure. He began doubting his commitment to this idea.

"Well, there is room for some changes here, I think," Alex began timidly. "We could perhaps start with just one or two of these, and, depending how those go, roll them out to the whole company."

"Alex, this just doesn't seem feasible," responded Marlene. "I think your head's in the right place, but even if we start with just a few of these, how will we choose who gets to implement them? People will accuse us of favoritism."

"I also don't have time to manage something like this on my floor," Eric, the man sitting to Marlene's left, added. He stood up and addressed the room as he spoke. "This seems like too much right now, with our quarterly reports being so poor and the winter months coming up. I think we should focus on incremental improvements and see if we can recover enough there to get by until things improve." Several people nodded their heads in agreement.

Alex sighed. His plans had now fully derailed. No one seemed enthused at all about bringing innovation and creativity to their company. Even fewer cared that Alex had demonstrated a lot of courage and vulnerability to bring this idea to them. He had tried to show them a new side of his leadership that he had always wanted to present but felt too insecure to bring forth. It appeared that authentic self was not good enough for this group.

He glanced at Adam, who had his head down and was trying his best to disappear in his seat. Suddenly, Alex had an idea.

"Actually, Eric," Alex replied, "You won't need to manage hardly anything. None of you will." He addressed the murmuring group. "We're going to pick five people at random to each take on a project. The costs will be minimal, I promise."

"And," he turned to look at his son, "We'll keep everything from being invasive to you by having my son take over management of these projects as his new summer job!" He beamed brightly at Adam.

Adam's head shot up to glare at his father. The executives in the room all began talking at once, angrily voicing their complaints to Alex and one another. "You want to bring on an additional employee?" yelled someone. "This is even more favoritism!" someone else grumbled.

"When I wanted to recommend my daughter for a job, you said we couldn't make family referrals. This is even worse!" Eric said loudly, standing up and stepping forward. "This is clearly not right, Alex."

Alex's eyes widened at this display from his colleagues. What had happened? Where had he gone so wrong? He had thought that bringing Adam on board would solve these problems, not make things so much worse. But it had, somehow. Eric, Marlene, the whole group had gone from disapproving to furious in the span of a minute.

Alex himself could feel the fury building up inside himself, too. And he burst.

"Wait, wait, wait! Hold on just a minute!" he cried, lunging forward. "You all are the ones acting inappropriately, not me. Shouting at your CEO is unacceptable and highly disrespectful. I am your leader! I will not tolerate this display. We are in a meeting, a space of sharing ideas and discussing plans in a civil manner. So please be quiet and sit down." He directed the remark at Eric, who slowly lowered himself into his chair.

The Office Visit

Alex stepped back and adjusted his tie, clearing his throat. The room was quiet; you could hear a pin drop. He continued.

"Thank you. Now, I believe you all owe me an apology, and my son as well—" He turned to Adam, but Adam's chair was empty. Alex saw a flash of the entrance door closing to his right. Adam was gone.

Alex buried his face in his hands and took a deep breath. Great. Now he had alienated his son even more and ruined the big meeting. He pulled his head up and addressed Carolina. "Could you please step in and do your strategy presentation now? Thank you." Carolina nodded and stepped forward as Alex marched to the door, opened it, and followed Adam outside.

***

"Adam! Wait!" Alex called out to his son, who was approaching the curb on foot. "Don't leave!" Alex hustled to catch up to his son, who was walking with more determination than Alex had seen from him in a long time. He finally caught up to him and reached out to grab his shoulders. "Wait! Just hold on—"

Adam whirled around, his eyes blazing. "No, you hold on! I can't believe you did that to me in there! You said I'd manage some crazy projects that nobody likes, this summer? I already have a summer job! Why can't you understand that?"

"I do, Adam, I do," pleaded Alex. "I'm sorry. Really, I am. I just thought that you could help me solve this problem, and I'd be doing you a favor, too—"

"How?" stormed Adam. "How is that a favor to me? I'd have to quit my job, which would put the country club out one person this summer on really short notice. Plus, I'd be managing a bunch of people who know I'm there only because I'm the boss's son. That's a great way to start a career," he spat sarcastically.

"Well, wait a second. It would be a great help to you, Adam. I know you don't want to hear this, but you need to start looking to your future. Being a lifeguard isn't going to teach you management and strategy skills. And it certainly won't help you get into a great college," Alex argued.

Adam laughed. "Well, it's a good thing my coding camp comes with an early-round interview at Purdue in the fall! Heaven forbid I spend the rest of my summer earning some money I can save for college." He shook his head and turned, staring at his father who gaped at Adam.

"Why don't you trust me, Dad?" he said quietly. "I've never given you any reason to doubt me, at least not when it came to school and knowing my strengths. I get good grades, and I always do my chores. I've never even gotten detention.

"I've tried for so long to share my interest in coding with you, but you just … you don't seem like you care at all," he mumbled. "And why should I care about your stuff if you can't be bothered to care about mine?"

Alex inhaled sharply. He hadn't thought about it that way at all. He suddenly realized that he had deeply hurt his son, had been hurting him for years, in fact. His heart ached.

He opened his mouth, but nothing came out. What could he say now?

Just then, a car pulled up to the curb. Adam checked his phone and the license plate, and waved to the driver. He turned to Alex.

"I called an Uber. I thought it's best if I leave," Adam said. Alex nodded, unable to speak with the lump in his throat. Adam pocketed his phone, gave a little wave, and hopped into the car. Alex watched as it sped off.

Once the car was out of sight, Alex broke down in sobs. Had he learned anything from Mike, or was what he was learning useless, good only in a conversation, but not real life?

He pulled out his phone.

"Mike, I know this is unscheduled, but I just blew it big time. When can we talk?"

Chapter Six

VISION

Alex sighed as he walked up to Mike's front door and rang the bell. It had been a tough few weeks since his disastrous company meeting. Adam was barely speaking to him, choosing instead to walk out of the room or walk in the opposite direction whenever Alex tried to approach him. Beverly was upset, too. She berated Alex for a full two hours once he came home, shouting about his lack of awareness and how he was "destroying the family from the inside out." Alex privately thought Bev was being overly dramatic, but he wasn't about to say that to her face.

The door opened, and Mike appeared, extending his hand. Upon seeing Alex's slumped shoulders and drawn face, he let out a low whistle. "I take it the meeting did not go well," he said quietly.

"No, it did not," Alex replied, shaking Mike's hand and entering the large foyer. "I tried. I really did. I just don't get what went wrong."

"Well, these are not easy lessons to learn," Mike said gently. "I'm not surprised you had some difficulty trying them out. It takes time!

"You've also only learned two of the five qualities it takes to be a COVETed leader. The one we're going to talk about today – vision – will help illuminate the path you need to take to avoid major distractions and problems. It comes from having a purpose in life that guides you in work and in life. Let's head to the patio." Mike guided Alex outside.

***

"So that's what happened," Alex sighed. He had just finished recounting the whole business meeting disaster to Mike, complete with his showdown with Adam in the parking lot. He even mentioned crying alone after Adam had left in the cab, which he loathed to do but figured it was best in the interest of full disclosure.

"That's really tough, Alex," Mike reached out a hand and clasped his shoulder. "I can see how painful it is for you to tell me this. I appreciate your personal vulnerability here. What happened to you was tough! As we talk today, I think I can pinpoint a few of the reasons why it didn't work out."

"I hope so," grumbled Alex. "I feel like I'm ready to make big changes, but I just can't seem to put it all together. I feel like a failure."

"You are not a failure," Mike stated firmly, looking directly at Alex. "You've simply had a setback. It happens to us all. But if you have a strong vision for what you want to accomplish in life, the major setbacks within our control are minimized. Difficult life circumstances can also teach us incredible life lessons and help us focus on what's really important. Vision begins with clarity."

"Clarity meaning…?"

"Clarity and simplicity of purpose, especially in times when you feel overwhelmed. A little clarity around your purpose can mean a mile of confidence. You have to be crystal clear about your purpose, your plan, your goal, and your boundaries. You're the leader. It's up to you to define a purpose for your organization and set expectations for your employees, like you do with your kids."

Alex stiffened. "Purpose?"

"Yes, the purpose for which your organization exists. It's about some cause, a belief. A belief about why the work you do is important. An inspirational *why* that employees can relate to, because people want to know *why they do what they do*. I hope you have a defined purpose statement for your organization, or don't you?"

Alex shook his head with an expression that was a combination of disbelief and resignation.

"I mean we have a mission statement," he said.

"Tell me what it is."

Vision

Alex looked at him blankly. "I don't know. I can't remember it. It's on a plaque in the lobby." He blushed.

"Don't worry. I can count on one hand the number of CEOs and employees who can recite their mission statement," Mike said. "It's symptomatic of the company culture. They don't know why they do what they do other than to collect a paycheck or have a career.

"The reason you had a chaotic board meeting was because you weren't linking your initiative to the purpose for which your organization exists. If you don't know what you stand for, or why you do what you do, trust me, your staff and employees and company officers don't either. You're the leader. They follow you, your passion, your reasons, or they make up their own, which may have nothing to do with what your intents are.

"By the way, let me warn you that making profit is not a purpose. That's just the outcome. Purpose should be broader in scope, something that makes you get out of bed in the morning, looking forward to going into work. It should be something that people care about. It should make your employees think, feel, and connect enthusiastically with each other and act from the inside out.

"Clarity of purpose precedes mastery and success. Any initiative that you introduce must have a direct link to the purpose that allows your organization to adapt to changes and iterate while not letting the central focus get blurred. An organization without a purpose *manages* people and resources, but an organization with a purpose *mobilizes* people. It mobilizes them because with purpose, people have a shared belief, a shared cause. The whole organization is aligned when people embrace a purpose that truly matters to them.

"If you have a clearly defined purpose, Alex, maybe you could even capture Adam's attention. For all you know, even he might embrace a worthy enough purpose."

Alex was beginning to shake inside. There was so much to integrate, to learn, to master. Would he be able to do it? "I can," he thought. "I can." He looked back up at Mike.

"Now what?" he asked.

"I think you're going to need to invest time and effort in developing and defining a *purpose* – a compelling narrative that sets the tone for a corporate culture – and make it mainstream. An actionable idea across the organization that binds them together. Build a culture around the purpose by rewarding purposeful behaviors, making every message and every action of the organization reflect the purpose. Set expectations that are communicated clearly and strongly. If your employees get the slightest whiff that you're not committed to your expectations, you'll fail. Boundaries around purpose lead to clarity. Clarity leads to focus, focus leads to attention, and attention leads to results and success."

Mike turned away from Alex and began to walk through the house. He stopped in the kitchen, opened the refrigerator, and grabbed a fresh pitcher of lemonade and two glasses. He turned towards the living room and continued to talk as he walked ahead of Alex.

"Clarity of purpose is the starting point of all success, and as they say, 'the best way to predict your future is to create it.' But you have to be absolutely clear where you want to go and believe in it with such conviction that it becomes a contagion."

He set the lemonade on the coffee table, handed Alex a glass, and motioned for him to sit down. Then he poured both glasses to the rim.

"Now, I want to tell you another story. I know, I know," Mike laughed, seeing the resigned look on Alex's face. "In fact, this time I want to tell you two stories. It's another one! But I want you to do something a little different when you listen to this one.

"I want you to focus on how this story might teach you something about vision, particularly what your own vision is for your life and your family. But I also would like for you to think about how it fits in with some of the other stories and lessons we've discussed so far. I want you to broaden your thinking a little bit. How does this reinforce the tenets of courage? Of optimism? How is it similar to Wangari Maathai's story, or Becky Blanton's, or Rose Mapendo's? What else can it teach us that may complement the lessons these incredible women have taught us?"

Vision

Alex thought for a minute. "I can do that. The five pillars are all related, so I'm assuming the stories share a lot of common ground, too."

"You got it!" encouraged Mike. "I like to think of stories as the building blocks for how we experience the world. Anyone can impact us at any given time, but their true power lies in how we combine them, new and old, to help us refine our values and beliefs over time. In the stories we've talked about, all of those women were courageous. They all stayed optimistic in the face of incredible hardships. And they all exemplified vision, excellence, and trust – the final three pillars of my COVETed leadership system.

"The first story is about a dear friend of mine from India. He was the CEO of a large manufacturing company that decided to expand by collaborating with a large Japanese company and diversifying their products range. The senior management of the company was very excited about the collaboration and got really busy with the details of setting up different plants and production lines.

"The message that the management spread throughout the manufacturing plants about the existing operations was that the Japanese technology would take everything to a different level of efficiency and how the company would become the biggest company in India.

"He told me that in his company there was no corner where you could not see signs of Japanese management techniques like 'Just-in-time,' 'Kaizen,' 'Six Sigma,' etc. The management took great pride in having these posters and banners put all over the place. Management was excited, but the employees were not. The mood in the company was very gloomy, and the workers and the frontline management were distraught, angry, resentful. My friend told me that the tension eventually reached a point where the senior management got really concerned. In fact, he told me of an incident when a visiting delegation from Japan had come to visit one of the manufacturing plants. One of the workers there spilled a large quantity of oil on the shop floor. So this friend of mine decided to call a meeting of the supervisors and frontline managers.

"He was angry about what was happening, so he addressed everyone in a very aggressive tone and came right out and asked, 'What do you think is the problem, and does anybody have a question?' I remember vividly he said that one new frontline manager was courageous enough to raise his hand and politely asked, 'Sir, do you really want to know the truth?' The CEO, getting angrier by the minute, said, 'Of course, why do you think I called this meeting?' The youngster said, 'Sir, the neck of the bottle is always at the top.' And when asked to elaborate, the employee said that the senior management was so busy with their own narrative and so caught up in their own vision and plans and shouting Japanese supremacy that they failed to remember that this was supposed to be a partnership. It was supposed to be a collaboration. The Japanese would not make any progress without the support and help of the Indian workers with their local experience. A simple example the employee gave was that the 'semi knock-down kits' that the Japanese were supposed to send would have been reduced to a thousand pieces in their original packaging had their Indian counterparts not cautioned them of the conditions of the roads in India. The CEO was flabbergasted and went back to change the entire campaign from one of Japanese supremacy to Indo-Japan collaboration.

"Now this particular story contains three very important traits necessary for establishing clarity," Mike said. He leaned back into the couch cushions and sipped his drink. "Other than having a compelling and contagious purpose, you need to be aware of these three traits because they establish clarity.

"First of all, you have to 'overcome biases.' In this case, the biases developed when management undermined and took the power of local talent and experience for granted and failed to recognize them, or the value they brought to the project.

"Second, 'be willing to iterate.' The minute the employees spoke to the CEO, he immediately decided to make amends. To his credit, and his leadership skills, he immediately changed the tone of the campaign. He set aside his ego and did the right thing. He listened to his employee's feedback and saw he'd been wrong.

"Third, in order to get the Indian teams to collaborate with the Japanese, the management team built in 'intrinsic rewards' by clearly giving them an equally pivotal lead role in forging the partnership."

Vision

"Wow," Alex said, as his jaw dropped in awe.

But before he could recover, Mike said, "Now let me tell you about the second example. This story is about a woman named Oseola McCarty. Oseola was born in 1908."

"The last time the Cubs won a World Series! That's a long time ago!" laughed Alex. "Glad we broke that curse!"

"Well, as a Cardinals fan, I can't say I'm too happy about *that*," grumbled Mike. "But I guess one every one-hundred plus years is enough."

"Hey!" Alex poked Mike good-naturedly. "You gotta give us one this century!"

"Fair enough!" Mike chuckled. "Anyway, Oseola was born in Mississippi and raised by her grandmother, mother, and aunt. They were poor, but had a tight family unit. They often relied on each other to make ends meet, even little Oseola. She would frequently come home from elementary school and iron clothes while the other three cleaned houses, cooked, and cleaned and folded laundry.

"One day, when Oseola was in sixth grade, her aunt was hospitalized and became unable to walk. This meant she could no longer do most of the work that had helped support her family. She also needed someone to care for her. So Oseola dropped out of school to be her caretaker and to work full-time as a washerwoman. She never returned to school.

"From that moment on, Oseola McCarty worked and saved nearly everything she earned. She had been taught early on by her mother and aunt the value of a dollar saved. With her mother's help, she opened her first savings account at First Mississippi National Bank, not long after quitting school. She had a vision and she was clear about it. She knew exactly what path her life would take and what she had to do to get there. She was clear, committed, and dedicated to her vision."

"Teaching kids how to save money is so important," sighed Alex. "Bev and I have tried to do this with our own kids for years, but I guess we're not the best at this either."

"It's tough, especially when considering things that would not have been a concern to Oseola. Education being one of the biggest. College isn't cheap!" replied Mike. "Even so, Oseola took frugality to a whole new level. Imagine working as a clothes washer for decades. Think about the paltry amount of money she earned, even accounting for rising wages and inflation. Do you think she was able to save that much without having a purpose or a plan for the money?"

"Probably not. I can't save if I don't have a goal or plan for it. Even then, it can be tempting to dip into it," Alex said.

"Exactly. But Oseola didn't. She retired in 1994. At the time, she was…"

"Eighty-six!" Alex exclaimed. "Holy smokes! Assuming she started working full-time at twelve years old, she would have worked for seventy-four years. That's incredible!"

"It truly is," remarked Mike. "What's even more incredible is how much she saved over the course of those seventy-four years. Tell me, Alex, how much do you think she was able to save?"

"Hmm," Alex thought out loud. "Well, you said she saved nearly everything. Assuming her wages were pennies to the dollar early on, and given the prices I saw at dry cleaners in my younger days, I would say, realistically, over time she could have saved a few ten thousand dollars? Maybe close to $40,000?"

"Good guess," said Mike. "If we were talking about someone who was good at saving money. Oseola was *exceptional* at it. It was her one true purpose in life, and she was willing to work incredibly hard to save as much as she could."

He opened his notebook and flipped to a page, pointing his finger, and scrolling down. "Here's what she had to say about work and purpose later in her life. 'I knew there were people who didn't have to work as hard as I did, but it didn't make me feel sad. I *loved* to work, and when you love to do anything, those things don't bother you. Sometimes I worked straight through two or three days. I had goals I was working toward. That motivated me, and I was able to push hard. Work is a blessing. As long as I am living, I want to be working at something. Just because I am old doesn't mean I can't work.'

Vision

"Now. Given *this* new information, how much money do you think Oseola saved during the course of her life?"

"I'm guessing several more thousand than my first estimate," laughed Alex.

"Try several *hundred* more. When she retired, Oseola McCarty had $280,000 in her bank account."

Alex whistled. "That is literally unbelievable. How did she manage to do that?"

"It's true, I'm telling you. She wasn't married and had no children. She didn't own a car and never traveled. She walked to get groceries, and her friends gave her a ride to her local church every week. In 1947, her uncle gave her the house she lived in until she passed away in 1999. Heck, she even considered a newspaper subscription an extravagant expense!

"But Alex, that's not even the most remarkable part." Mike leaned forward. "Upon her retirement in 1994, Oseola decided to give it all away."

Alex blinked. "All of it? To whom?"

"Well, she divided it up. Ten percent went to her church, and ten percent went to each of her three surviving relatives. The other sixty percent – this is interesting. It went into a scholarship fund at Southern Miss. Osceola specifically stipulated that these funds should be used for students who could not afford to attend otherwise, and preferably those of African-American descent."

Alex nodded enthusiastically. "I see! So she was trying to ensure that what happened to her didn't have to happen to other young people from less fortunate circumstances who wanted to get an education."

"Yes," said Mike, "And she knew she wanted to do this since she herself had to leave school at age twelve. She made a goal – to work hard and save as much as she could so others could have a better life – and focused on it exclusively for the next seventy-four years. She created the circumstances under which she and others could succeed. This takes incredible clarity and vision to accomplish."

"I'll say!" said Alex. "That's some incredibly powerful vision she had!"

"Definitely," Mike agreed. "I like to think of vision this way. It's the ability to see the unforeseen. In many cases, it can help you spot the iceberg before your Titanic hits it. In Oseola's story, she had to overcome many obstacles, adapt, persist, and work incredibly hard to avoid potential Titanic-like poverty and increased costs of living.

"But vision is a lot like courage and optimism. When people see it in their leaders, it inspires them to behave in a similar way. Wangari Maathai inspired women in Kenyan villages to fight against unjust environmental and economic conditions, using optimism and positivity. Elizabeth Lesser inspired countless men and women to own their courage and deeply connect with those who matter most to them. Holding true to your vision will help inspire others to see what you're seeing – your beautiful future.

"Oseola's incredible story and her generosity inspired others to support those who could not afford education. Her donation to the university sparked a fundraising drive that raised over $330,000 from more than six hundred donors. And, after hearing of Oseola's gift, Ted Turner himself gave away a billion dollars to the United Nations."

"No kidding!" exclaimed Alex. "That is really big! Is that what they used to start the United Nations Foundation?"

"Yes! That's the gift that started it all," replied Mike. "And Miss McCarty kept inspiring people for years after this gift was established. One of her traveling companions described it this way." Mike once again flipped through his book and read from a page in the middle. "People treated her like a monument. But she was really a movement. A movement that will keep moving."

"Wow," said Alex, trying to absorb everything Mike had just said. He had often thought of the company he was building and his plans with Adam as moving towards a greater vision for his life and his family. But after hearing Oseola's story, he was starting to realize that his so-called vision wasn't so forward thinking. In fact, it seemed more focused on immediate needs. Alex's desire to get Adam involved in the family business had been top of mind, but he hadn't considered what might happen once he accomplished that goal. How would the company grow? And what about the rest of his family? Was his vision too singular?

Mike observed Alex deep in thought. He asked quietly, "What's on your mind?"

Vision

Alex sighed and leaned back, crossing his arms over his chest. "I was just realizing my own vision is pretty small," he admitted. "I really thought I was thinking ahead and planning for my family's and my company's future. But the truth is I haven't thought much beyond convincing Adam to get on board. I should be doing a lot more succession planning and thinking about David's future and—"

"Whoa, whoa," laughed Mike. "Slow down there. Oseola's story is incredible, and her vision inspired a lot of good in this world. But don't think you have to suddenly start making grand plans to create a better future. Remember, Oseola started small, but she was consistent. She clarified what her purpose was and dedicated her work and life to fulfilling that purpose, day in and day out. Tell me, Alex. What is your purpose?"

Alex looked at Mike. "Well, I thought it was to provide the best life I could for my family and my employees."

"That's a great purpose!" exclaimed Mike. "You want to work hard and live your life to the fullest, so those around you can benefit in multiple ways. Financially, sure, but also from your hard work, your experience, your joy, all of it. That's serving others from your heart." Mike placed his right hand on his chest. "But you're allowing yourself to lose focus from this purpose."

"How so?" asked Alex, his brow furrowing.

"Well, think about Adam. You said your purpose was to provide the best life you could for your family and employees. Now, you have interpreted that as bringing Adam on board to be involved in the company, maybe run it one day. But have you asked yourself if that's what would give *Adam* the best life possible?"

Alex opened his mouth and stopped. Mike saw a look of realization cross his face. He continued.

"And if you were to bring Adam on board, in a job he doesn't seem very passionate about, would that be great for your employees and their lives at your company? You have to keep your purpose top of mind, always. Your purpose should be your driving force and should be contagious, not repulsive."

"I thought I was," confessed Alex. "But listening to you talk, it's starting to click. I've been pushing Adam towards a future I want for him, but it may not be the future he wants. If I try to make him do what I want, the whole system kind of collapses, and no one's happy."

"That's a great way to think about it!" encouraged Mike. "Think about your own body and the systems required to keep it working optimally. Everything's gotta be working together in order for the whole system to function at its best."

"But it's so easy to get distracted or for things to go wrong," groaned Alex.

"Absolutely! Vision is tricky in that way. We have to be flexible and adaptable; things can and will go wrong. Situations will arise all the time that can distract us from our vision. It can twist our reality and move us far off track if we let it. This reminds me of another story. Have you ever heard of a man named Isaac Lidsky?"

Alex thought for a second. "I don't think so."

"He's a young man who's done a little bit of everything. He graduated from Harvard at age nineteen with an honors degree in math. He served as a law clerk to two U.S. Supreme Court justices. He lost his sight to a rare genetic disease, and he runs a construction company in Orlando. And oh, he starred on a television sitcom."

"Wow, TV?" Alex inquired. "What was the show?"

"That is usually the first question people ask him," laughed Mike. "It's called *Saved By the Bell: The New Class*. It was on for several years in the 90s. It's interesting that we tend to focus on the glamorous and more positive aspects of a person's life. Tell me, what did you feel when I mentioned his blindness?"

Alex hesitated. "Well, I definitely felt uncomfortable. It must be tough living with that kind of disability, so I guess I felt some pity, too."

"Hmm, a common response," said Mike. "But what he's learned from his blindness is actually a far greater vision than his eyes could provide alone.

"Isaac wasn't born blind. He lost his vision progressively, from age twelve to twenty-five. He describes the change as being in a 'carnival funhouse.' He mistook mannequins for store employees; he couldn't make out shapes in clouds;

objects seemed to morph once he felt them or others described them to him. And then one day, he couldn't see at all."

Alex winced. "That sounds devastating."

"I'm sure it was, in a sense. Your visual cortex takes up about thirty percent of your brain. Every second, your eyes can send the visual cortex as much as two *billion* pieces of information. The rest of your body can only send your brain an additional billion, at most. So your sight is responsible for about two-thirds of your brain's processing resources. Over the course of twelve years, he lost that resource completely.

"But what he learned while this was happening was that sight can be an *illusion*. To create the experience of sight, your brain doesn't simply send and receive signals. It actually references your conceptual understanding of the world, your memories, your opinions, emotions, attitude, pretty much everything you *think* you know to be true. And these connections work both ways. What you see can affect how you feel, and how you feel can then change what you see. Have you ever heard someone who has committed a crime talk about 'blacking out' while they were doing it?"

"Yeah, definitely," replied Alex. "Usually pretty bad stuff, like murders or beatings."

"Those tend to be the most covered cases. But that's an example of how our vision is not strictly objective. A hill might appear steeper if you've recently exercised. An SUV may look bigger parked next to a small car than when parked next to a Hummer. What we are seeing is actually the reality we've created, but one we experience passively as a direct representation of the world around us.

"Many of us lead our lives in such a passive way, taking our reality at face value and not recognizing how our assumptions, opinions, memories, and histories affect how we view the world. Isaac's debilitating disease taught him this. Though he initially thought it would be a death sentence for him, he learned to face his fears and *see* them as fictions we perceive as reality.

"Think about your relationship with Adam. You think your reality with him is that he's stubborn about joining the family business and not as motivated to learn the *right* skills to prepare him for a successful career. But is this Adam's reality?" Mike sat back and crossed his arms. "I bet if you asked him, he'd share a much different view."

Alex sighed. "I bet you're right. And from his view, I'm a pushy father who never listens."

"Have you ever shared with him why you have this vision?" asked Mike. "Not from a practical point of view, but from your heart?" Mike put his hand over his heart. "You have hopes and fears, as we all do. Adam does, too. Not confronting those fears, and not creating your own reality around your dreams and vision, is preventing you from truly connecting with your son. Isaac calls these 'backwards-swimming fish.' Here's what he has to say about them."

Mike pulled out his trusty notebook and read from a passage in the middle, "In your career and personal life, in your relationships, and in your heart and soul, your backwards-swimming fish do you great harm. They exact a toll in missed opportunities and unrealized potential, and they engender insecurity and distrust where you seek fulfillment and connection. I urge you to search them out." Mike closed his notebook and looked at Alex. "So what are your backwards-swimming fish?"

"Well, certainly my fear of losing Adam," admitted Alex. "I'm also afraid of letting him fail. I have regrets in my own life about skills I should have learned earlier and jobs I should have taken. I didn't apply myself in college, and I feel like I paid for it later in life."

"And those fears are now impacting how you handle your relationship with Adam," interjected Mike. "You're trying to make up for the mistakes of your past with your own son."

Alex slowly nodded his head. "Saying it out loud, I think that you're absolutely right."

Mike smiled. "So let's turn this into a positive. Let's focus on how you can train your brain to help you execute your vision, how you can build intrinsic rewards for Adam and clear this ambiguity.

"If you want to cultivate the ability to see the unforeseen and create your own reality, first you have to establish clarity in your purpose. You have to overcome the various biases that exist in your life. In your case, most immediately, this

Vision

means overcoming the tendency to equate your past misgivings with Adam's present circumstances, and as I said, it is absolutely imperative that Adam find intrinsic rewards in that vision. He can't just see the external rewards you have been using as a bribe. The minute a better offer, or bribe, comes along, you'll lose him. There has to be an intrinsic hook, something he can't get elsewhere, for it to work.

"It also means shutting down the negatives, and the voice in your head that says, 'I can't do this.' You can! And you have many times in your life. I promise you. Tell me, can you think of a moment when you defied your own expectations for what you could accomplish?"

"When I saw Adam riding his bike on his own for the first time," Alex replied immediately. "As soon as I saw him take off and pedal faster and faster, I thought, 'Bev and I have actually raised this kid and taught him things! He's learned from us!' It was an incredible feeling."

"I can definitely relate!" agreed Mike. "I have amazing memories of teaching my own kids to ride their bikes. It truly is an awesome feeling to watch them go out on their own.

"What I want you to do is hold onto this feeling. Keep it clear in your mind. It's obvious this is a powerful feeling for you. But it won't be easy. Remember when we talked about optimism? You have to force positivity in your own mind a little bit. The negative feelings, the fears, the biases, can creep back in without us realizing. It takes some mental discipline to achieve this.

"This becomes particularly problematic when we hold an 'intrinsic bias' about something. We may try to make ourselves believe something we know we should believe, but we will still react quite differently or, in fact, in a totally opposite way. We just can't seem to change the way we act if the new belief is inconsistent with our internal belief. I remember I once had a head of operations, Joe Dunn, in one of my companies. He always spoke highly of one of his subordinates, a young girl named Jane Riley. I still remember her name.

"She was very smart and hardworking, and she had taken up quite a few assignments aimed at improving efficiency. She always looked like she had a promising career ahead. During one of our talent management exercises, Joe had brought a list of names to the committee as prospective candidates for a vacant position of a unit head. I was very surprised that Jane's name was not on the list, and during the meeting, I looked at Joe and asked why he didn't think that Jane could be the candidate.

"He had a totally astonished expression on his face as though he was asking me 'Are you serious?' And when asked to explain, he realized that he had a huge *internal bias* against having a female unit head. His bias existed despite the fact the company was a totally equal opportunity employer. It had not even occurred to him that a woman could be given the position of the unit head, and he was totally unaware of this, as this bias resided deep in his subconscious."

"And it took some courage to admit it, I'd imagine," Alex said.

"Absolutely!" Mike beamed. "You have to be courageous in your pursuit of your vision and really lean into it. Joe and others have done it, and you can, too.

"This brings me to the second tenet of vision: finding comfort in discomfort. This can mean many different things. For you, Alex, part of it is recognizing that failures will happen, but they don't signify a failure *at life*.

"You have to get comfortable with being uncomfortable in moments like you experienced a few weeks ago in the boardroom. You need to manage the ambiguity that will get created around your vision and make others realize that the positive difference that the new initiatives make—of course being driven by the *purpose*—is going to be much greater than the discomfort. Failure is a part of everyday life, something I think you try your hardest to avoid and bury.

"I'm not just speaking from experience, but from research. Did you know that researchers tested volunteers' memories by showing them images which were rated as novel, familiar, and very familiar? What they learned was that when people were shown something novel, something outside their comfort zone, and then a familiar image, their memory was better," Mike said.

"Meaning?"

"Meaning that while repetition helps us develop good memory, mixing in new information, things that push us into the novel or uncomfortable realms, are important. When we do something new or different, something that makes

Vision

us uncomfortable because it's unfamiliar, our brains are triggered to release dopamine, nature's natural happy chemicals. Here's the kicker. That part of our brain is only activated when you see or experience completely new things. Moreover, success will not come to you. You will have to go and find it."

"Seriously?"

"Seriously. It's why I only hire managers and executives who have extensive travel experience or who have lived abroad. I know they've dealt with new countries, new airports, stressors, and consistent discomfort. They have to find their way around, deal with language problems, adapt, change, be prudent risk-takers and operate at high levels of stress. Their brains, their creativity, and their problem-solving grows as a result."

Alex thought about what Mike was saying. It was true. His own extensive travel experiences made him a much better executive for just the reasons Mike was describing. His multiple failures at navigating new cities, asking for help, and being willing to take calculated and prudent risks had made him more resilient and taught him a lot of lessons.

"Instead of erasing or burying your failures or memories of failures, think of failure as an opportunity to grow and refine your plan for your future. Always be willing to iterate your plan. Adam may not want to work for your company, but that doesn't mean you can't provide a great life for him. It means you need to adjust and adapt.

"Another way of finding comfort in discomfort is to really dig in and work *hard* for what you want. Oseola McCarty is a perfect example of this. Her washing work was not easy. She didn't use a washing machine. She washed and pressed all of her clothes by hand. The labor was *intense*. But she took comfort in knowing that this hard work would enable her, her family, and others from similar circumstances to have a better life."

"She did it for so many decades, too," reflected Alex. "It puts my own work into perspective!"

"It certainly does!" agreed Mike. "I've often thought about the discipline required to do what she did. We talk about work ethic and perseverance all the time in business, but Oseola's story really highlights the importance and possibility of those ideas in a new way.

"Come on into the kitchen. Today I'm going to treat you to something very special," Mike said. He waved his hand, pointing for Alex to have a seat at the open kitchen counter. "I'm going to treat you to some special Indian tea."

"Ah! That'll be great." Alex sat down on the tall stool and leaned forward, his forearms resting on the marble countertop as he watched Mike.

Mike pulled a glass teapot from the cabinet, poured two cups of water in it, and put it on the stove. As the water started to boil, he pulled a can from the cabinet and removed some special tea leaves. He dropped them into the teapot and motioned Alex to watch. "Get a little closer. I want you to watch this," he said.

Alex obliged, standing up and walking over to peer into the teapot. "Boiling leaves," he said. What was he supposed to see?

As the tea leaves boiled, Mike turned to Alex and asked, "What do you see happening?"

Alex watched for a few seconds. "Total turmoil, kind of a mayhem, leaves moving all over the place, kind of knocked around by the water, coming up to the surface, then down again," Alex said. He watched the tea leaves colliding, unfurling, and almost dancing as they continued to move topsy-turvy in the pot. Mike threw in some ginger and a few cardamom pods. The water kept boiling, unlocking a unique intense aroma. Alex loved the smell and said, "I can't wait to taste it."

Mike poured some milk in the pot and said, "This is Indian tea, one of my refreshing secrets. But what I want you to watch is what is happening in the pot."

Alex peered over Mike's shoulder and said, "Looks like there's a mini-storm in the pot."

"Exactly," said Mike. "That's exactly the reaction I wanted to get from you." Alex stood there a little confused. Mike continued, "Out of this chaos and discomfort you're experiencing comes a perfect aromatic tea. That's what happens with any discomfort. Once you learn to endure the discomfort, the end result

Vision

is clarity, new learning, and growth. When you step out into the unknown and leave the harbor of the known, you will feel discomfort, but if you are intentional about making the change then you will be equipping yourself for bigger and better success. The opportunity cost of not venturing into the discomfort is grave, and when you find the strength to endure the discomfort, the gain is always worth the pain."

Alex sipped the tea and said, "Wow! This was definitely worth it." He winked at Mike. "I mean it was worth putting those tea leaves through the discomfort."

Mike smiled as both of them settled to savor their tea.

"Oseola and Isaac," Mike continued, "were able to persevere because they worked through the hard stuff completely. In other words, they *avoided the path of least resistance*. This is an incredibly important tenet of vision, and something I don't think a lot of people understand.

"Have you ever gotten an email promising to teach you the secrets to owning your own business in ten minutes a day? Or the articles advocating for a three-day work week?"

"I get a lot of those in my inbox," confessed Alex. "I don't sign up for most of them. I did at first, but then I learned even the legit ones never really seemed to work for me. I tried one that promised to help streamline my email efficiency to ten minutes a day."

"Did it help?"

"No. I just got really behind on replies!"

Mike nodded. "Those kinds of tips promise a quick fix to a much deeper, unidentified problem," Mike noted. "Having trouble writing a presentation or analyzing data? Here are twenty exercises to focus your mind! Want to be more efficient at work? Do a four-hour work week. That will really force you to get it all done!"

Alex smiled broadly, then sipped his tea. "I take it they're not your favorite either."

"Usually not," Mike replied firmly. "Efficiency tips and focus exercises have their place, but they're too often used to mask the real problem: people taking the easy way out of a situation involving hard work and reflection. Why do people take the path of least resistance?" Mike leaned forward. "It's because they have a fear of failure. But if they let go of the past or let go of the fear, then they are able to go and do something bigger than themselves – find a purpose bigger than who they are.

"Experiences are simply opportunities for people to learn. This is one of the biggest points I've been trying to make to you." Mike shared clasping Alex's shoulder with one hand,."You, Alex, are not a failure. You can fail, sure; but *you* are not a failure. You must learn to forgive yourself. You are *enough*." He squeezed Alex's shoulder.

Alex blinked, once again holding back tears. He wasn't sure how Mike managed to evoke these kinds of responses in him, but it felt good to hear that from Mike. He was finally starting to see all the pieces fit together. What had happened at work, and between him and Adam, wasn't a condemnation of his roles as a leader and father. They were simply a part of life. It was up to him to look at them in the right way. They could be opportunities for positivity, success, courage, and action, not markers of failure. They could enable the future rather than take away from it.

Alex looked at Mike, who was watching him intently. "I think I'm beginning to get it," he said quietly. "I can't conflate what I've done with who I am, or who I will be, or who anyone else can or should be. I have to look at things differently or else I'm going to keep sinking."

Both sat in silence for a few minutes. Then, Mike spoke. "That's a powerful realization you just had. How does it make you feel?"

"Really good, actually," Alex responded. "It felt great to hear you say I was enough. I guess I never thought about it that way, at least not lately, but I *am* enough! We all are. Adam especially. He's a great kid, and I need to communicate better with him. I need to listen more. I have to take some prudent risks with Adam and believe that nothing bad will happen. I need to learn to manage this discomfort because the reward at the end, or the difference that this approach of engaging Adam and seeking his help in managing my relationship with him, is definitely going to be much larger."

Vision

Mike beamed. "This is a wonderful breakthrough, Alex. And I think you realize, too, that it won't be easy, but the difficulty is a beautiful part of the journey on its own. That's also the next lesson I want to share: you have to overcome the tendency towards expediency. Much like avoiding the path of least resistance, we all have to understand that the fastest and easiest route to life is almost always a failure – short-term gain for long-term pain.

"Now, this doesn't mean that you won't have short-term successes along the way. We need the balance of success and failure to ensure we're constantly tuning our vision and focusing on the right values and goals. But over time, you must recognize that persistence is focus's first cousin. You must keep the important things in your vision at all times. As Goethe once said, 'Things that matter most must never be at the mercy of things that matter least.' I actually have this engraved on a small stone on my desk. I look at it often, to remind myself of my own path and vision for my life."

"That's a beautiful quote," agreed Alex. "Very succinct. And very direct, too."

"That's what I like about it," Mike said. "There's intention behind the statement. Although it's written in a passive voice, it's clear that *we* are responsible for prioritizing those things that matter most. It takes will-power and persistence to keep your sight focused on long-term wins. Life is a marathon, not a sprint. It's cliche, I know, but it's true. Short-term rewards can be a great temptation. Too many businesses fall prey to the temptation for instant rewards. They are too hungry for instant gratification.

"We have often seen that near fatal mistakes occur in their businesses. But staying persistently connected and committed to your long-term goals, asking questions like 'Is this decision or move going to distract me or take me closer to the long-term goal?' is what guarantees solid rewards. The key is you need to enjoy the ride and not get impatient by delays, no matter how long or how many. Mark Twain once said, 'The secret to success is making your vocation your vacation.'"

Mike abruptly stopped talking and looked at Alex, as if he could read Alex's mind. "This is all good talk, but reality is something else. I can't tell what you are thinking, Alex, but I am saying this for two reasons. One, to make you think and reconsider what you have been doing with Adam, and the other is to help you on your job. I am going to explain that with a story.

"A very great friend of mine makes movies. He is a film producer. He once invited me to visit him on his sets. Have you seen any film shooting?"

"No."

"Well, it's definitely not as exciting as the movie itself. The day I visited they were to shoot a midafternoon scene. It was late morning. The sun was still not at its peak, and this was out in a desert. When there was no action, while the cast and crew were all there, I asked him why the shooting was not taking place. Much to my surprise, he said they were waiting for the sun to be right on top. I asked him, 'How does it matter? It's still very sunny and hot.'

"You know what he said? 'If I wait for the sun to shine the brightest today, I will have it shining brighter for the rest of my life.' I found that so profound," said Mike.

Alex was struck dumb and could hardly speak, but managed to utter "Amazing."

"This brings me to the final tenet of vision," Mike said. "Adaptive intention. We must be purposeful in the decisions we make, but we must also be flexible enough to adapt to new situations.

"Let's say you are walking down the street, and there is a pole in the middle of the sidewalk." Mike stood and began to demonstrate. "You need to shift your walking path so you don't hit the pole. You use what is taught to fighter-pilots, OODA: Observe, Orient, Decide, and Act." Mike ticked each one off his fingers as he spoke. "You observe what's coming; you orient your thinking and your location; you decide what needs to be done; and you act to do it.

"This may seem obvious, but it's less so when you're in the middle of a tough decision. An easy decision is like walking towards the pole at a natural rate. A tough decision is like speeding towards the pole at ninety miles per hour. There are outside factors that can make OODA more or less difficult.

"Like staying positive, being courageous, or acting with purpose. You have to train your mind to use OODA in more complex mental, physical, and emotional situations. This is about putting yourself in a responsive versus passive position when making decisions that can outmaneuver competition.

"Wayne Gretzky said it best, 'To be a winner, you don't skate to where the puck is, but you skate to where it will be.'

"The window of opportunity in OODA is very narrow, and you need to act on it quickly. This is most required when you are at critical crossroads in your life, and acting with OODA could really change the outcome in a quick go-no-go situation. The reason OODA could have such long-lasting and far-reaching impact is because it is steeped deeply in moral will and skill, prudence, and emotional intelligence."

"These leadership qualities really do require discipline, focus, and practice to get them ingrained in your mind," observed Alex.

"They certainly do! That's why none of these are a quick fix. But their power lies in this persistence and focus. I'm not saying you have to be born with innate qualities to be a leader. Quite the opposite! Hard work, courage, positivity, vision, and focus can help you achieve your goals and be the leader you want to be. That's the beauty of the system.

"What's important is that you can't just rely on the left hemisphere of the brain. That's your rational, sequential, and logical brain. It's doing all the analytics. You also need a strong reliance on your right hemisphere, the nonlinear, intuitive, and emotional brain. It's the side of your brain that does make the *what feels right* moves. You have to bring into play the wisdom of both moral will and skill. Moral will and skill give us the ability to use wisdom in a practical way that calls for improvisation when the situation demands. You must be present in the moment with it. There are no shortcuts. You have to experience it all and be committed to it."

Alex nodded. "I knew that about the brain," he said. "I just never thought of applying it to something like leadership, or moral will."

Mike took another sip of tea and then set his cup down. He reached for the pot and poured himself another cup.

"Let me tell you about an interesting book I read," he said. "It's called *The True American*, eloquently written by Anand Giridhardas. It's a true story and beautifully written. It captures the essence of moral will and raises some thought-provoking questions. He writes, ten days after 9/11, a tattooed man entered a Dallas mini-mart. He held a shotgun at Raisuddin Bhuiyan, a Bangladeshi immigrant working at the register and asked, 'Where are you from?' Raisuddin had been robbed before and knew what to do. He quietly put cash from his register on the counter and stepped back. But the man didn't touch the money. Instead he again asked Raisudden, 'Where are you from?' Raisuddin was confused. He said, 'Excuse me?' With only two words, his accent betrayed him, and the man, a self-styled true American vigilante, shot Raisuddin in revenge for 9/11.

"Dozens of scalding birdshot pellets from the shotgun punctured Raisuddin's head. The shot didn't kill him, but he lost his left eye. He was rushed to the hospital only to be turned away because he did not have insurance. He lost his job. His fiancée left him, and he ended up with $60,000 in medical debt. He had gambled everything to come to America, the land of opportunity, and he had lost it all.

Mark Stroman, the shooter and vigilante, born in the land of opportunity, had failed to take advantage of what could have been. A product of bad parents, bad schools, and bad prisons, Stroman was arrested even before he had shaved, thus starting a life cycle of prison, violence, and hatred. A white supremacist who became a vigilante eventually found himself on death row after his 2001 counter-jihad rampage where he had shot not one mini-mart clerk, but three.

Only Raisuddin survived. Both men's stories could have ended there, but they didn't. Raisuddin had gone on a pilgrimage to Mecca, once there, he remembered that in 2001, as he lay dying in, he had promised God that if he lived, he would serve humanity. He decided expressing his gratitude for God's letting him live and survive the attack would best be expressed by giving the man who shot him, a man now on death row, a second chance at life himself.

Raisuddin wasn't the only one reflecting on his life. Stroman also got a second chance to change. While in prison, he spent time in introspection. Gone were the violent criminal friends he'd spent his life with. Now he was in the company of virtuous and caring pastors and journalists. They listened to him, prayed with him, and helped him quit his old influences and bad habits. Ten years after the shooting, Stroman heard that Raisuddin, the cashier he had shot, was fighting to save Stroman's life.

"Raisuddin felt immense gratitude for his second chance at life, no matter how tortuous it had been for a while. He felt a *moral duty* to intervene and stop this cycle of vengeance.

"In the name of Islam and mercy, he publicly forgave Stroman and then went on to sue the state of Texas and its governor, Rick Perry, to stop Stroman's execution.

"His unprecedented act of mercy and forgiveness was inspired by his moral will. As he learned about Stroman, he decided that Stroman was the product of poor upbringing, a broken home, and bad company. So he testified in Stroman's defense, appealed for clemency, sued the state, and even spoke to Stroman in the jail. He said, 'Mark, you should know that I am praying to God, the most compassionate and gracious. I forgive you, and I do not hate you. I never hated you.'

"His best efforts failed. Stroman was executed. But Raisuddin wasn't deterred. After the execution, Raisuddin, who was still committed to operating out of moral will, reached out to Stroman's eldest daughter, who was also an ex-convict and an addict, and offered his help."

"Wow," Alex shook his head. "I don't think I could have done any of that."

"That's why moral will is so powerful," Mike said softly. "Not many can act out of morality. It has to come from a place deep inside us, a place that recognizes our humanity and that of others. It's something you develop over time, under tremendous pressure, through courage and faith."

Both men sat quietly, thinking about what it must have taken for Raisuddin to do what he did.

"I think I underestimated this part of it," Alex admitted. "I've been pretty successful in the later part of my career, and it's come fairly easy to me. I mean, I've had to work hard, but I could see the path pretty clearly, and I was able to execute it without a lot of pain. But changes are coming more quickly now, and more frequently. I just didn't get that to truly be happy I might have to change my mindset and adapt."

"Absolutely," Mike said. "A wise person knows exactly when and how to make an exception to every rule. As they say, to change one's mind is rather a sign of prudence than ignorance."

"Prudence?" inquired Alex. "Like we discussed under courage?"

"Yes," Mike said. "The ability to look reality squarely in the eye without allowing your emotion or ego to get in the way. In fact, some people argue that's the most undervalued trait of leadership today – to be able to detach yourself from any prejudgment or bias and look at any situation in its wholeness while being emotionally intelligent.

"Those qualities will not just help you become a great leader, they will also help you become a happier, smarter, more compassionate, brave, agile, and empathetic person. Business improvements are great, but they don't mean a whole lot if the person leading them isn't happy or pursuing his vision with all his heart.

"For the next time, I want you to think about these tenets of vision: clarity, comfort in discomfort, avoiding the path of least resistance, overcoming expediency, and adaptive intention. Persistence is key. How can you practice these every day in your interactions with Adam and in your business dealings?

"Remember, we're not looking to boil the ocean here. Keep it simple and straightforward. With Adam, focus on *him* and his interests, what actually drives him, what his purpose is, even if you don't understand it. Ask him about the things you don't understand. I'm betting he'll enjoy being the expert just as much as you do. What does he like to do? What are his interests? How does he like to communicate? You'll need to keep at it, and you'll need to be adaptive. And don't forget to lie in your courage and stay optimistic! It might be expedient to just force him to think, do, or act a certain way, but you'll lose him. Lose the expediency factor."

"Is that all?" groaned Alex, laughing. "That sounds like a lot!" He did have to admit that if he focused on individual interactions, it didn't seem that bad.

Vision

"You'll adjust to it, I promise," said Mike. "Just remember to be patient and kind with yourself. If you ever need any encouragement, feel free to give me a ring. I'm always happy to chat!"

"Thanks, I appreciate that," said Alex, relieved.

"Anytime," Mike smiled. "Now, a toast." He produced two champagne glasses and a bottle of champagne, and filled both to the brim. He passed one to Alex and raised his own in the air. Alex followed suit.

"To you, Alex. May you always hold your vision in the darkest of days." They clinked their glasses and took a sip.

IN SUMMARY:

The five pillars of Vision are:

- **Establish Clarity.** Clarity is not just a clear vision. It's a clear vision plus the one hundred percent commitment to that vision by the leader. Not only must the vision and commitment be clearly identified and communicated by the leader, but the language, process, and protocols must also be so clear that it becomes a contagion. The leader must build and make others see intrinsic rewards in the purpose, set boundaries, and use committed language. NOT "I'll try," or "We'll try," or "Let's see how this goes." Don't be distracted by biases, but use and enforce positive language. Say "We will." As the saying goes, "Let your yes be yes and your no be no." Nothing kills a vision or clarity more than an indecisive leader. There may be times you might have to reiterate, but be intentional even while making adjustments.
- **Find comfort in your discomfort.** No one likes discomfort, but it's the only way we grow. Studies show we grow best when pushed beyond our comfort zones, or when we deal with something unfamiliar, uncomfortable, or unknown. Business expert Seth Godin wrote, "Discomfort brings engagement and change. Discomfort means you're doing something that others were unlikely to do because they're hiding out in the

comfortable zone." When you are uncomfortable and yet take prudent risks that lead to success, the organization rewards you and brings you back for more. There will always be an element of ambiguity, but by being willing to ask for help and moving ahead with the conviction that nothing bad will happen, you lay the foundation for success.

- **Avoid the path of least resistance.** The path of least resistance is the safest, most comfortable, and easiest path. And that is exactly why it should be avoided. It's not only the easiest. It's usually the most mediocre path. We all fall into the mediocre trap because it is difficult for us to avoid the fear of failure, especially if we have had a bad past experience. But if you want to make a difference, you need to let go of the past and see experiences as learning opportunities. Forgive yourself for your failures. Believe that you are *enough* and that you will succeed if you persevere. R. W. Emerson said it best, "Do not go where the path will lead you; go instead where there is no path and leave a trail."

- **Adaptive intelligence.** Adaptive intelligence is the capability to use information for convenient reasons, including being able to communicate with other people, to connect with and educate yourself on your surroundings, climate, or culture. It's the moral will and emotional intelligence to be able to look beyond self, to notice and absorb information about what is happening around us, and then adapt to perform better, do more, or come up with solutions based on prudential judgment, i.e., taking counsel carefully with our own self and others, judging correctly from evidence, and then acting based on norms that emerge. It is foresight and far-sight, the ability to take immediate decisions on the basis of long-term effects.

- **Overcome the expediency factor.** Expediency is not a virtue; it's a vice. In spite of what many managers and business owners may think, getting things done regardless of how it impacts people, teams, businesses, or the public is not a good thing. 'Task Completion Bias' will only bring short-term gain for long-term pain. Short-circuiting the process will only distract you from staying on course. It is important to remain

Vision

focused on what is truly important, to be attentive and aware of issues and challenges, and to be persistent no matter what challenges come up. When you persist through your determination and willpower, then you don't just achieve success, you *become success*.

Chapter Seven

EXCELLENCE

"Thanks, guys," Alex waved as the last of his strategy team walked out the conference room door. The afternoon's planning session had gone very well, especially once Alex had turned the reins over to a young executive named Paula.

Paula had been with the company for six years, but her growth had stagnated a few years ago and it had mystified Alex, until recently. After the disastrous company meeting, Alex vowed to listen to his co-workers' concerns more carefully and consider their views before making significant internal changes. He was now drawing everybody's attention to the *purpose*, not just his plan.

Paula had come to one of Alex's new "open door" sessions and expressed a strong desire to lead, citing several new initiatives that could improve workflow and help the company attack their strategic initiatives more powerfully.

In fact, many employees like Paula had taken advantage of the opportunity to chat with the big boss. Alex couldn't believe how much they had been bringing to the table lately. Clearly, he had needed to implement changes much earlier, but, he reflected, under the old Alex's vision, he never could have been so vulnerable or willing to listen.

His open door sessions were one of many programs, large and small, that Alex had recently put in the pipeline at his company. He had developed them using Mike's COVETed leadership principles – the three principles he'd learned so far, anyway. They were all designed to foster a more authentic, joyous work culture, and a clearly defined and embraced purpose. He wanted to empower people to be the best version of themselves at work, and to feel valued for their contributions. Alex was beginning to learn that if he wanted this for his coworkers, he had to show them courage, compassion, optimism, and his vision for success in return. He had to take ownership of his values and show the employees they could trust him with their work and their ideas.

He walked down the hall and saw a few folks from the marketing and data analytics department chatting around the coffee maker. They were laughing, clearly enjoying a break from the hustle and bustle of the day. Alex remembered seeing them a few times in the past and dismissing their chatter as idle. But now, he saw an opportunity to connect with people, to learn what they valued and what excited them. He headed over.

James, one of the lead data analysts, waved when he saw Alex heading over. "Hey, Alex," he greeted him, a surprised look on his face. "We don't see you by the water cooler much! What's up?"

"Hello, Mr. Johnson," piped up a shorter woman standing right behind James. Alex recalled that she had once given a wonderful marketing pitch at an executive meeting earlier in the year. She was poised and confident, and her proposal had been incredibly well-researched. Cindy, was that her name? Whatever the case, he also remembered he hadn't taken the time to tell her what a great job she did. No time like the present.

"Hi, James. Hello, Cindy," he reached his hand out to shake hers and waved to the others. "Please, call me Alex. And I just want to say, in case I missed it before, how great your presentation was earlier this year. I know we've moved it through to execution. How's the project coming along?"

"Oh, great!" exclaimed Cindy, clearly a little flustered by the praise. "We've begun building out the mockups, and we should be ready to launch the campaign in a month or two. Grigor's been a great associate lead," she gestured to the man standing next to her. "And the analytics team has given us some wonderful data to better frame our campaign. In fact, this partnership has been so useful, we've been talking about creating a guide that other departments can use to better utilize the data and resources James and his team can provide."

Excellence

"That's excellent!" Alex replied, amazed. "What a great idea! I'd love to hear more about this. Are you guys able to stop by my office tomorrow, maybe in the afternoon?"

Cindy beamed, and James nodded. "Sure. Should we make an appointment with your secretary, or...?"

"No, no," Alex waved his hand. "Stop by any time after 2pm. If that doesn't work, feel free to call me directly, and we can get something on the books. My door is always open."

"Sounds great. We will do that!" replied Cindy.

The group chatted with Alex for another ten minutes, sharing news about their day and relaxing over coffee. As Alex said goodbye, he noticed he felt invigorated by their conversation.

"Funny," he thought, "in the past just thinking about making small talk with my coworkers would fill me with dread and anxiety." But he had to admit that he'd enjoyed hearing about their lives. Who knew James was into drones? And Grigor loved wine? He'd also enjoyed sharing more about himself with them, too. He had apparently never told them about his love of skiing, or his travels with his family to places like Italy and Japan. Adam especially had loved Japanese culture and begged his parents to take him back as soon as possible.

Speaking of Adam ... Alex suddenly had a thought. He turned and looked back to the group.

"Hey James, do you have a second to chat real quick?"

"Sure," replied James, walking over to Alex. "What's up?"

***

Later that night, Alex turned into the family living room. He had just finished shooting hoops with David on the driveway. Bev was in the kitchen, chopping vegetables for dinner. Adam was lounging on the couch in front of him. Remembering his conversation with James earlier, Alex took a deep breath and approached his son.

"Hey, Adam. Do you have a sec?" Alex asked, sitting beside Adam.

"Sure," sighed Adam, snapping his laptop shut. "What's up?"

"Well, I've been thinking a lot about what happened between us a few weeks ago. I first want to apologize."

"Dad, it's fine," Adam said, protesting.

"No, it's not," Alex insisted. "I was way out of line in proposing that you join the company this summer. I should have asked you first and respected your right to make your own choice."

Adam blinked. "Oh, um, thanks Dad. I appreciate that." He nodded his head. "I really do."

Alex nodded back. "You deserve nothing less. I know I haven't really listened to you in the past, but I want you to know I am trying. Now, I may not always get it right," he laughed. "I still don't really understand much about coding, and you're my oldest, so a lot of this is new territory."

"I know you might not get it, Dad," Adam responded. "I just want a chance to learn more about it without feeling like I can't do anything with it, you know? Like I have to do only what you want me to do."

"That's totally fair," Alex agreed. "And I haven't allowed you to really explore your interests on your own. I've stopped you from doing that, actually, in some cases. So I'd like to make up for it."

"What do you mean?" Adam sat up, interested.

"I found out earlier today that one of my associates, James, has an interest in drones. He's considering building a few models and has drawn up some plans and code for them. This is still very early in development, but I told him about your interest in drones and he said he'd love to chat with you about what he's learned so far. No pressure, of course," Alex added. "This isn't connected to my company in any way."

"Wow, really?" Adam brightened. Alex could tell he'd piqued his interest. "Yeah, I'd really like that. Thanks, Dad!"

"No problem," Alex smiled at Adam. "And who knows, maybe down the line you'd be able to work for him and—"

"Whoa, whoa, Dad!" laughed Adam. "You're doing it again. One step at a time!"

Excellence

Alex chuckled and held up his hands. "You're right! I'm sorry. Old habits die hard." He reached out and grasped his son's shoulder. "Just remember to listen to James. He works in data for a living and knows all about coding, and drones are a big hobby of his. There's a lot he can teach someone who's new to coding—"

"Dad," interrupted Adam. "I'm not really that new to it. And I'm actually pretty good at it, too. If you don't believe me, you can ask my teachers and my coding camp counselors. And you can see my public repository on GitHub," he grumbled, shrugging his shoulder out of his dad's grasp.

"Oh," remarked Alex, uncomfortable. He had crossed a line, but he wasn't sure exactly what the line was. "No, I believe you, son. I'll tell James to reach out to you over email if that works.

"Okay," Adam responded, nodding his head. He paused, then looked at his dad. "Thanks. I'm … I'm really looking forward to it."

"I'm glad I could help," Alex smiled at Adam. He stood, gesturing towards the kitchen. "Now, how about we go help your mother with dinner? I'm famished."

"I can do that," Adam replied, rising up and walking towards the kitchen ahead of his father.

When they both reached the kitchen, Bev handed Adam a spatula. "Can you stir the potatoes, please?" she asked. As Adam turned to oblige, Bev leaned into Alex. "I heard your conversation," she whispered. "And I'm proud of you, sweetheart." She beamed at him and kissed him on the cheek. Alex grinned.

"I told you I've learned a lot from Mike!"

***

"You sure seem happy!" exclaimed Mike when Alex bounded out onto the patio. Mike stood to shake Alex's hand, then both sat in their now customary seats. "I take it the homework went well?"

"It's going really well actually," Alex affirmed. "I've thought a lot about what you said during our last session. I've been trying to keep my vision front and center, and work through discomfort and resistance to make it happen. In doing that, I realized how much I had been avoiding *connecting* with people. Especially Adam. I thought taking the time to chat with coworkers over coffee, or talking about anything with Adam besides his future, was a waste of time.

"But I realized work came easier, and my family seemed closer, when I was honest with them and myself about my vision. I had to live in the moment to make those things happen, too, which was a new experience for me! I'm used to thinking at least five steps ahead."

"That's a great observation!" Mike declared. "Living in the moment is a key part of being courageous, optimistic, and having vision. It's also absolutely crucial for being your most authentic self."

"It wasn't easy," Alex admitted. "And I still find my mind drifting when I'm stressed or not paying attention."

"It can be difficult to train your brain to be present," Mike agreed. "We're so used to tuning out these days – our phones, our email, social media, any kind of product we can imagine – it's all available to us so immediately. We rarely take the time to just *be* anymore. But we need to if we want to lead our lives as richly as possible."

Alex nodded his head vigorously. "I can see the difference already when I do pay attention, versus when I don't. I think I just need to build up my endurance and resilience for it."

"You do, certainly. Think of it like weightlifting. You can't walk into a gym and pick up two fifty pound weights and do fifteen reps for five sets just like that." Mike snapped his fingers. "You have to practice. Remember what we talked about with vision? Don't choose expediency. Persistence is focus's first cousin."

"I've been saying that phrase a lot in my head lately," Alex said.

"It's a good one! I've found it's gotten me out of trouble more than once in my life," Mike replied.

"Persistence also relates to what we're going to talk about today – excellence. This is the fourth pillar of the COVETed leader model, and one many of us often take for granted."

Excellence

"I'm afraid I may have done that with Adam earlier this week," Alex sighed. "I'm not entirely sure what happened, but I think I underestimated or questioned his skills in coding."

"Tell me about it." Mike leaned forward. "What happened?"

"Well, I offered to set him up with one of my tech guys for an informal chat. Adam's been very interested in coding and drones, and one of my colleagues just so happens to be starting a side venture in these areas. So I thought if I connected them, Adam could learn a thing or two," Alex said.

"That's great!" replied Mike.

"I thought so, too. But when I said that my colleague could teach a newcomer a lot about coding, Adam got very defensive. He started telling me about all these people and places that could vouch how good he was at coding, and I wasn't sure how to respond to that. So I just let it go."

"Hmm," mused Mike. "Sounds like you hit a sensitive spot there. Does he talk a lot about coding?"

"He does, actually," said Alex. "I didn't even realize it either, until I started really listening to him. He writes a lot of code in his room, stuff that can work with drones and other flying technology." Alex gestured his hands in the air. "He attended a coding camp earlier this summer and apparently it was invite only. Bev said he excelled at nearly every challenge they threw his way."

"That's great!" exclaimed Mike. "He seems like he is working towards excellence as I want to teach it to you today. Excellence is the ability to know and do what you are good at, and be the best at what you do. Adam clearly knows he's great at coding. He is doing it and trying to be the best he can be at it.

"Now, notice the definition isn't 'the ability to know and do what others think is impressive.' Excellence comes in all forms and applies to whatever captures someone's passion and drive. You can be an excellent bartender, executive, father, street sweeper, little league coach, daughter, personal assistant, husband, model train enthusiast. Whatever you *do* in your life, you can and should practice excellence in it. COVETed leaders recognize this and apply excellence to all areas of their lives."

Mike leaned forward and looked at Alex directly in his eyes. "I would say where you ran into trouble with Adam was in failing to recognize his trying for excellence, or even potential for excellence, in *his* chosen area. You may not value coding and drones, but Adam *does*. COVETed leaders not only see the excellence in themselves, but they see it in others, regardless of what it is they do."

Alex sighed. "I know it's something he values, and I believe that people can make a great career out of coding and development if they apply themselves the right way over time. But Adam's only sixteen, there's no way—"

"Alex," Mike interrupted. "Excellence is also not only about the end goal. You're thinking too far into the future again. Remember, *be present*." He reached out and grabbed Alex's shoulders and shook them lightly. "Adam can be excellent at coding *now*, as long as he is adhering to the five tenets of excellence. I'm going to share those with you today."

"Okay, fair enough," Alex said. He felt his reluctance and resistance rising. He could see how being in the present was useful for courage, optimism, even for developing your vision. But how could excellence just *happen*? He asked Mike, who chuckled in response.

"I hear your skepticism. And you're right, in a sense. Excellence doesn't just happen overnight. It requires lots of hard work and discipline. And like anybody who strives for excellence, I think I can explain it to you. Let me tell you—"

"Another story," Alex finished in unison with Mike. They both laughed, and Alex lifted his hand and gestured for Mike to continue.

"So," began Mike, "Have you ever been to Johannesburg, South Africa?"

"No."

"There is a man who works at the Johannesburg airport who epitomizes the pursuit of excellence. What do you imagine his job is?"

"I would guess he's the director of the airport, or one of the executives on the board? Maybe one of their financial guys?"

Excellence

"Good guesses. But you're wrong. It was actually…," Mike paused, taking an extra long sip of his iced tea. Alex squirmed a bit in his seat. He knew Mike was making him wait for effect. What could it have been?

Mike noticed his discomfort and smiled before continuing, "… a janitor."

"A janitor? Really?" Alex raised his eyebrows. He looked bewildered. "How does he best represent excellence?"

"He represents excellence because he loves his job. He uses it to express his best self, and he makes the world a better place because of it," replied Mike, ticking each reason off his fingers as he said them. "When you walk into that bathroom, you see an extremely clean space and a man who greets you with kindness, charity, and love, shouting, 'Welcome to my office!' He talks to you. He asks about your day and tries to make it better by providing the best custodial service he can. And he's always looking for ways to improve.

"Many have passed through his office, and they have all benefited from his commitment to excellence. It didn't matter what his position was, or that he didn't have a fancy title or executive-level list of accomplishments. He excelled at his job. He knew it, and he performed it to the best of his ability."

"It sounds like this fellow has made quite a difference!" replied Alex. "How do you know about him?"

"I met him on a trip to Madagascar. This was maybe seven or eight years ago. I had organized a ten-day aid mission through my foundation, and I was flying with twelve volunteers from my company. We had a layover in Johannesburg, and our second flight ended up being delayed over four hours. We had a boat to catch right after we landed, and time was already tight. So naturally we were all a little panicked.

"I went into the washroom to freshen up and gather my thoughts. I felt stressed, out of control, worried. But as soon as I walked in, I was greeted with this happy booming voice. 'Welcome to my office!' I turned and saw this guy, and I ended up chatting with him for nearly twenty minutes, about my troubles and pain, and his work and what it meant to really care for what you do. That whole time, I never saw him neglect a customer, and I never felt neglected in turn. He truly cared about his work on a professional *and* personal level." Mike shook his head.

"I'd never seen anything like it. When I left the washroom, I felt so much calmer and sure of myself than when I'd entered. I had seen before me someone who truly excelled at his job. And I was determined to provide that same level of excellence in leadership for my team."

"Wow," remarked Alex. "That sounds like a really powerful experience!"

"It truly was," Mike affirmed. "When I came back to the group, they could see immediately that I was calmer and confident in our cause despite everything going wrong. My calmness calmed them down. We could all enjoy the trip and focus on our mission. We ended up arriving exactly where we needed to be. The trip was a great success!

"It sounds weird, but the change this gentleman had made was simple but profound. He put so much of himself into his work that it had an echo effect. After talking with him, I wanted to excel. I felt like he wanted me to excel even though that topic never came up. I wanted to know and do what I was good at, and be the best at what I do. I wanted to inspire others to be the best, too."

Alex nodded. "I can see how excellence begets excellence in this case. The fact you're still talking about this story shows how much of an impact he had on you."

"And I'm not the only one," responded Mike. "If you search online, you'll find many folks who have run across this gentleman and been affected by his work excellence. Tweets, articles, photos. Robin Sharma, a motivational speaker, even made a video of him. He described him as 'working like Picasso painted,' and I couldn't think of a better take. He truly took as much pride in his work as any artist or philosopher would."

Alex laughed. "The comparison between Picasso and a janitor is quite…"

"Incredible? Unbelievable, in the truest sense of the word?" Mike laughed. "It may seem that way, but that's what the pursuit of excellence should bring out in all of us, the ability to be our own Picasso."

Excellence

"I know Picasso was a great artist, but wasn't most of that natural talent?" wondered Alex. "I mean, I'm sure he practiced and all that, but can we really expect to achieve as much?"

"Oh, Picasso was a notoriously hard worker," Mike replied, picking up the iced tea pitcher and refilling both of their glasses. "Did you know his library of work includes 1,800 paintings, 1,200 sculptures, 2,800 ceramics, and 12,000 drawings? That doesn't even include the countless prints he did on rugs and tapestries." Mike paused, while Alex was struck dumb.

"I had no idea," Alex said.

"Most people don't," Mike said. "There's a story about a woman who once spotted Picasso in a market. She got very excited, and she approached him, asking if he would do a sketch of her that she could keep as a souvenir. Picasso agreed. He took out a piece of paper and sketched the woman in only thirty seconds, complete with her name and his autograph. The woman was overwhelmed to see it was a masterpiece. He had captured her, unmistakably, with that trademark Picasso flair. She rolled up the sketch and started to walk away.

"'Wait,' Picasso said to the woman. 'My fee is $10,000.'

"The woman was shocked. It was a thirty second sketch! 'I'm sorry, but you must be joking,' the woman responded. 'You spent thirty seconds on this and now you want $10,000?'"

"I can understand her disbelief," agreed Alex. "I mean, he is Picasso, but that wasn't an art auction. It might be worth that nowadays, but when he was alive? In a market? No way."

"Well, from Picasso's view, through all his hard work and his commitment to excellence, he'd earned the right to charge that amount. As he told the woman, 'It took me thirty years' of practice to do that sketch in thirty seconds.' Excellence doesn't come overnight. We cannot rely on talent alone. Picasso certainly couldn't. You have to work for it, and work for it hard."

"Okay, when you put it that way," Alex admitted, "thirty years is a long time to pay your dues."

"Exactly. Remember, with excellence, it's about *knowing* what you're good at, doing it, and being the best at it. Picasso hit all of those marks because he practiced his craft day in and day out. Because of this, he knew what he was worth and asked for it," Mike explained. "And this bore out long after he passed. How much do you think that quick Picasso sketch would be worth today?"

"Probably millions," Alex guessed.

"That's what I think, too," agreed Mike. "Picasso's dedication to his craft beautifully represents the first tenet of excellence: consistency.

Picasso was exceptionally prolific throughout his career. He created thousands of works of art, in many different styles and media forms. He was able to do this because he worked hard to master his craft. He focused on creating every day, and creating *well*. The same goes for the janitor in Johannesburg."

"Okay," said Alex slowly. "But there are people every day who work very hard trying to create something amazing. Not everyone can be at the top. So how can we pursue excellence knowing not everyone can succeed?"

"It's not about everyone trying to get to one place or to be the best or number one. Excellence means different things to different people. Excellence, and the consistency required to achieve it, come from focusing on your *virtues*.

"There's a behavioral economist named Dan Ariely who performed a fascinating experiment on this. He had a group of students assemble Bionicles, these little toy figurines made by Lego. He then divided them into two groups. For one group, the students could display their Bionicles on their desks and assemble as many as they wished, but they were paid a very low amount for assembling the figures. Nevertheless, these students reported feeling very productive seeing them all lined up on their desks. They continued building them, even though the pay was low and the task itself was not especially meaningful.

"The other group was instructed to give their completed Bionicles to a supervisor, in exchange for another box of parts to assemble. The supervisors immediately disassembled the Bionicles and gave the parts back to the workers for assembly. Each group was paid the same for the work, according to a scale that began at $2.00 for the first figurine and decreased by $0.11 for each one assembled thereafter. "Now, how much harder do you think the first group worked than the second?"

Excellence

"Hmm," Alex thought. "Well, both were paid the same amount, but my guess is the first group made more because they could keep the product of their hard work."

"You would be correct!" agreed Mike. "Those who were allowed to keep their assembled figures built an average of 10.2 figures. Those whose work was disassembled built an average of 7.2."

"That's a pretty significant difference! I didn't think it would be that big. So the second group would have required more incentive to make more figures?"

"Yes. In the American workplace, we typically incentivize workers with money. But these students would have required forty percent more pay to equal the output of the first group. Forty percent! That's the value of following your virtue. We can't hope to equal those kinds of numbers if we just focus on the financial reward." Mike smacked his hand on the table. "That's why consistency is so important. If aligned to your virtues, it can lead you to excellence."

"And it didn't matter what they were creating, so much as the fact that they were creating something *they* found valuable," Alex added.

"That's it!" Mike affirmed. "They, the janitor, and Picasso all worked consistently to produce the best work they could, because they *believed* in what they were creating and mastering their craft. In fact, the consistency they showed in their work was not the result of any cognitive practice but, in fact, the result of a certain disciplined behavior that guaranteed sustainability.

"Let me tell you about my visit to a pharmaceutical company that was run by a friend of mine. While on a tour of the shop floor, I had a chat with a worker who was in charge of sterilizing the bottles for the cough expectorant that the company manufactured. I noticed he was being obsessively meticulous with the cleanliness of the bottles. I stopped and asked him why was he being so obsessive.

"And his reply was so deeply rooted in the values the company promoted while also appealing to the workers. He said, 'This cough syrup is an over-the-counter drug that would be dispensed by any pharmacy anywhere, even without prescription. It could so happen that this cough syrup might get distributed to the area where I live. My wife could buy it for my kids, and if there was something hygienically wrong with the drug, my kids' lives could be in danger.' That was such a profound truth and value-driven response that it left a mark on my memory forever." Mike paused for some time and sipped his green tea before continuing.

"You see, Alex, in order to play to perfection, you will need to master your craft, no matter what it is. You can't make half-hearted attempts. People who excel work purposefully and raise the bar every day by becoming their own competition. I read somewhere that 'impossible is the new possible.' I wondered how true that was, but then I thought, unless you bring a better version of you each day, you are not actually living, because there is no living without growth. I hope I am not sounding too professorial," Mike joked.

Alex smiled and said, "No, not at all! In fact, that is the point I was perhaps trying to make the other day in the management meeting. The reason we have slipped in our position in the market and sales have dropped is because we haven't brought in any new initiatives that would help our guys raise the bar." He paused for a few seconds. "I guess, as you said, I should have linked it to our purpose and drawn the connection to the mastery of craft."

"Absolutely", said Mike, "You have to appeal to the moral duty of dialing into the vision and doing what is right by helping your team to reason the difference between the greater good and the discomfort of change, and when that happens, they also demonstrate the next tenet of excellence: grit."

"Digging in and playing hard," Alex said. He sighed heavily as though grit were a dirty word.

"Why the long sigh?" asked Mike. "You're right, by the way. Grit *is* about working hard and playing the game, but it doesn't have to be so negative. Angela Duckworth calls it persistence with passion. Sounds more fun, right?"

"Yes, it does, but well, this is where I find it hard to reconcile optimism and excellence. If you want to dig in and play the game, as you say, that comes with a price," Alex said. "You have to answer to all the critics and naysayers that also want to play. It's really hard to practice optimism in the face of all that."

"I agree," Mike said. "I never said any of this would be easy! But it's not impossible to reconcile. You don't have to answer to those critics, Alex. That's

Excellence

where focusing on your virtues comes into play. Hang on, there's a famous quote from Theodore Roosevelt I want to share with you." Mike picked up his notebook and shuffled to a page in the back. "Here it is. It's pretty famous. You've probably heard it before.

"It is not the critic who counts nor the man who points out how the strong man stumbles, or where the doer of deeds could have done them better. The credit belongs to the man who is actually in the arena, whose face is marred by dust and sweat and blood; who strives valiantly; who errs, who comes short again and again, because there is no effort without error and shortcoming; but who does actually strive to do the deeds; who knows great enthusiasms, the great devotions; who spends himself in a worthy cause; who at the best knows in the end the triumph of high achievement, and who at the worst, if he fails, at least fails while daring greatly, so that his place shall never be with those cold and timid souls who neither know victory nor defeat." Mike closed his book. "There's a lot to unpack here. But I want you to focus on *why* the player is the only one who counts. He is the one out there, putting in the work, and doing it for a *worthy cause*. And what happens if he fails?"

"At least he's earned the respect of others?"

"He's earned his *own* respect, for himself," Mike answered gently. "And while that may not seem that significant, *it is*. It's where everything you do in life stems from, Alex. If you can't respect yourself, how do you expect others to respect you? How can you cultivate optimism, as you said? How can you develop excellence? Or vision? Grit helps you accomplish this more than anything else because you're working hard for yourself and aiming for perfection, even if you don't hit it.

"The hardest demons to battle are the ones you create for yourself. So, how do you combat that? You dig in and *work*. And, you learn, learn, learn. Relentlessly."

"Learn? You are big on learning, aren't you?" Alex said.

"Yes, of course. We are all works-in-progress. We must relentlessly learn anything and everything, and from anybody, related to the pursuit of excellence and how you want to excel in your life. In fact, the one who knows more, wins more. This is the next tenet: You should aim to improve at all times. Learning relentlessly and making incremental improvements will help you accomplish this," said Mike.

"How so?"

"Well, there are different ways of thinking, but it is this constant learning, this constant evolution, this constant curiosity and learning about new concepts and new ways of seeing the world that can provide you with the new perspectives that drive success. Perspective can help you see things in a different light," Mike explained. "Think about the Lego builders. If we just see the second group, building and rebuilding the same figurines, then we might think the only way to incentivize them to build more is to give them more money. But if we then observe the first group, we learn that there's a different way. We learn how to *value* the work differently. And that gives us incredible insight into improvement.

"All of these stories illustrate the benefits of constant and consistent improvement and the power of hard work. We must bust the myth of overnight success if we want to build a valuable life. We need to make incremental improvements and live in excellence every single day. It comes one small step at a time."

Alex nodded slowly. "Ok, so we should learn *what* every day?"

"Aim to learn substantively," corrected Mike. "Think about your dreams and goals. How can you learn in different ways to make those dreams bigger, better, more substantive?"

"I hadn't thought about the value of different perspectives in that way," Alex said, nodding his head. "But I can see how that would help boost your vision while quieting the naysayers in your head. I do find that I'm more negative when I'm stuck in one little area or in my own head."

"That's the beauty of perspective and excellence," said Mike. "Its effects are exponential. It can help you see yourself in a kinder, more respectful light. It can teach you new perspectives, thus sharpening your vision. It gives you courage, and it helps you stay positive and upbeat.

"Build a valuable life. In other words, connect with something bigger than yourself, something much nobler, something that goes beyond chasing your own career and material dreams. This will bring out the untapped talent and potential in you because what you do for a living will make you focus only on those skills that your work demands. Looking beyond your immediate work will help you expand your capabilities and grow exponentially, which will in turn help you see your workplace as your empire."

"That sounds totally worth it." Alex reached for his pen and pad and started scribbling notes.

"It certainly is! But to achieve that, you need deliberate practice, disciplined pursuit with laser sharp focus on your goals. The concept of overnight success is a total myth and absolute misnomer. Actual success comes from *ridiculous* practice, *crazy* hard work, and *obsessive* focus on improving. Improving your performance, your character, your behavior, your whole being.

"But in order to do that you have to follow two more tenets." Mike raised one finger in the air. "Settle for nothing but the best, and practice self-discipline. Nothing changes before you do. You have to decide that you are going to work for the best, and you have to hold yourself accountable to do just that. "Two." He raised a second finger. "Avoid procrastination, use your time well and honestly, and set your priorities.

"The janitor in Johannesburg could have done the bare minimum for his job. Picasso could have taken a more casual route to painting. But those men chose to challenge themselves. To continue with the game metaphor, they played to win. Ask yourself, Alex. Do you want to play to win?"

"Of course," Alex admitted. "I always want to win. I hate losing. I hate to be in the situation I was the other day. It was perhaps one of the worst meetings and may be the worst meeting this year at work, and then to make it worse, I had that showdown with Adam. That really killed me. I need to confide in you. I literally cried in the bathroom that day."

"Well, in that case, you will have to develop an unconditional and unstoppable commitment to winning and putting in your absolute best effort," said Mike. "There is no doubt you went into that meeting ill-prepared." Alex looked up at Mike and nodded.

"Alex, when you step into that meeting, people expect you to bring value. They expect you to awe them and surprise them. You can't afford to maintain a linear trajectory. But that doesn't mean you can fall into the 'I am not enough' trap and let those voices in your head sabotage your focus.

"I'm guessing you were perhaps too engrossed in making a quick impression that you cared about the dropping sales and the poor performance of the company. In the process of doing that, you failed to actually stretch yourself enough to do a comprehensive research to develop the proposal into something worthwhile. But that doesn't mean you can just give up and let your commitment, determination, and focus go awry. Remember, anything worth having takes time. You can't let reasons make the list and emotions make the decisions. You need to have an unwavering commitment to winning. Your focus determines your reality, and the single best determinant of success is your *preparedness*. You need to prepare absolutely well without trying to cram things up."

Mike got up and casually went over to the bar counter. He bent down while Alex watched him intently. He pulled out a large wide-mouthed jar and placed it on the table. He then bent down and brought out some large fist-sized rocks and placed them carefully into the jar, one by one. The jar filled up after he had placed a few big rocks. Then he turned to Alex and asked, "Is the jar full?"

Alex peered over into the jar and said "Yes," at which Mike said, "Well, let's see." He then pulled out a bag of pebbles and poured some pebbles into the jar, shaking it vigorously.

Again he turned to Alex and asked, "Is the jar full now?"

Alex hesitated for a few seconds and then said, "Yes." Mike smiled and said, "Let's see." Then he pulled out a bag of sand and dumped sand into the jar. It flowed smoothly into the spaces between the rocks and pebbles. When he finished he asked Alex again, "Is the jar full now?"

Alex finally understood what Mike was doing and said, "No."

"Excellent," Mike said. Finally, he grabbed a pitcher of water and poured water into the jar until the jar filled to the brim. Once again, looking at Alex, this time rather intently into his eyes, he asked, "What do you think the point is here?"

Excellence

Alex thought for a minute. "That there's always some room left for more?"

"Could be, but there's another lesson here," Mike said. "The bigger lesson is that the rocks are the things that truly matter in your life, the things you'll treasure at the end of your life, like family, friends, hopes, and dreams. The pebbles are the things that give the rocks meaning, like your friendships, love, hobbies, travels, and fulfilling personal goals."

"And the sand and water?" Alex asked.

"The sand and water are the things that fill our time up with meaningless tasks. Running errands, watching television, hanging out, or wasting time for no good reason. A good leader focuses on the rocks."

"Why?" Alex asked.

"Well, think about it. What would have happened if I had filled the jar with sand and water first?"

"There wouldn't be room for the rocks and pebbles."

"Exactly. If you're going to have a life filled with all the things that matter—friends, family, love, fun, travel, dreams, and whatnot—and have room for the day-to-day, you have to focus on filling it with rocks first, then pebbles, then sand and water."

Alex nodded vigorously. "I get it. Priorities."

"We only have 24 hours in a day. What we fill it with depends on us," Mike said. "Focus on the big things, the things that matter."

"Hmm, that's a powerful lesson," Alex said.

Mike added, "Well there is another lesson, Alex, remember your strategy meeting the other day, you failed to draw your team's attention to the big rocks, meaning your vision and the big picture and hence they all got distracted and drifted on to smaller and inconsequential discussions leaving no room to connect with the big rocks.

"So what are your rocks, Alex?"

"I don't know. I'm confused. Maybe the first rock is how I learn to better connect with Adam and be the best father, husband, and leader at work."

"It can absolutely mean that, if that's what you want," Mike offered. "Remember, excellence is defined by the ability to know and do what *you* are good at, and to be the best at *that*."

Alex nodded. "I get it. And that *is* what I want." He stood up. "I think I know exactly what I have to do in my organization and to bring this perspective into my life and Adam's life."

"Oh, yeah?" Mike grinned "Remember, nothing lasting can happen unless you get down to actually doing it." He stood up to walk his guest to the front door.

Alex nodded firmly. "Yes, I think I will bring along a guest next time, Mike. Is that okay?"

Mike grinned. "Absolutely."

IN SUMMARY:

Excellence is the ability to know and do what you are good at, and be the best at what you do.

The five tenets of Excellence are:

- **Improve at all times.** If something is not growing, it's dying. If you're not improving every day in some way, you're dying. And somewhere, someone willing to improve themselves in even the smallest way is passing you by. To remain a *freshman forever,* seek guidance from experts. There's a saying among runners that even the person who finishes last in a race always finishes ahead of the people who never get off of the couch to begin with. You don't have to be working on an advanced degree, but you can be building a valuable life by improving a subskill.

    You could be adding incredible value to your life and the lives of people around you by making incremental improvements. There's no overnight success. The only person who can decide how far you can go or stretch yourself is YOU. Your workplace is your empire, and you

Excellence

can plan to learn, grow, and improve your empire through deliberate practice and the pursuit of discipline.

- **Settle for nothing but the best.** Any winning coach in any sport will tell you that you must practice like you plan to play. You can't do something at half speed in practice and expect to play at full-speed in a game. How you work and what you settle for in your everyday life, in the smallest or least important task, is how you will work and what you will settle for in your major negotiations, under stress, in a crisis, or when you have the chance to seize an opportunity for yourself or your company.

  Nothing in your life changes without you, and no one is going to come and do your work for you. So stop playing short, and stop playing the victim. Make nonnegotiable commitments, hold yourself accountable, challenge yourself, and settle for nothing but the best from yourself and those you work with.

- **Grit.** Grit is simply courage and resolve; perseverance and passion that builds strength of character. It's discipline and dedication to being in the game longer than others. It's hard. People with grit have the ability and tendency to sustain interest in and make effort toward very long-term goals. Grit is resilience, the ability to stay so committed to the belief that there is no plan B. It's the ability to fight your internal saboteurs and bounce back after every failure and setback. It's an appetite for relentlessly learning, a burning desire to strive for excellence, an uncompromising resolve to seek, find, and never yield.

- **Self discipline.** Self-discipline is the ability to control one's feelings and overcome one's weaknesses. It's the ability to pursue what one thinks is right despite temptations to procrastinate. It's the ability to set priorities, to know what is important, and use time wisely. You cannot pursue too many things at the same time. You must prioritize and do things that matter most. Establish simple habits and rituals that make starting productive work and optimization of your energy natural and easy.

- **Consistency.** Consistency is the steadfast adherence to the same course, form, process, or actions based on virtues. It's doing the right thing as a moral duty, no matter the cost. It's not just about responding to crisis, stress, and challenges the same way or at least with the same mindset every time. It is also about the way you show up everyday in mundane moments, such as the way you behave in rush hour traffic or interact with a waiter in a restaurant, or for that matter, when no one else is looking.

Consistency is mastery of your craft. It's about exceeding expectations – not someone else's expectations but your own – by making mastery a behavior. When you focus on behaviors, your actions become consistent. You become mindful of the urges that keep you from giving your best each time, and you begin to commit one hundred percent to your obligations. People know or begin to learn what to expect. You consistently show up demonstrating virtues such as dependability, trust, self-control, humility, and honesty.

Chapter Eight

TRUST

Alex stepped out of his car and closed the door. He squinted up at the bright sun beaming down on Mike's driveway. It was truly a perfect day. Not a cloud in sight. This seemed fitting for his final session with Mike. He really wanted it to end on a high note for both men as well as for his special guest.

A few weeks ago, he realized just how much he'd come to treasure his time with Mike. Over the past several months, they'd forged a close friendship that rivaled any Alex had built in his life. He found himself looking forward to their monthly sessions. He'd even taken to replaying past conversations in his mind, recalling the many nuggets of wisdom Mike had shared and the kindness, tough love, and compassion he had shown while guiding Alex through the COVETed leader model. Alex could honestly say he had learned more from Mike than any leadership training course he had taken in his life.

One area that had greatly improved thanks to applying Mike's model was his relationship with his coworkers. He had noticed that lately they felt much more comfortable approaching him with new ideas, thoughts for improvements, even just to chat about their day. Alex felt humbled that it had taken him so long to see the value of a simple conversation. He had already allowed many of them to implement the programs and changes they suggested, with most taking direct ownership of their projects themselves.

Alex smiled to himself as he thought about Cindy, Grigor, and James's data analytics initiative. The group had identified six potential projects that would benefit from the data team's input. They had drawn up plans to facilitate the various partnerships and enjoyed it. He was impressed by how quickly they had moved on this venture. Alex was glad he had given them the reins and that he had trusted them to execute it without his usual strict executive oversight. He wouldn't have done that a few months ago, that's for sure.

Nor would he have seen the value in considering Adam's future as anything but connected to his company. Alex admitted that he was still working on this part. He still very much wanted Adam to join him. His company was his passion and his path, and he wanted to share it with his son. But he was beginning to see that Adam needed to forge his own passions and path in life. Alex should support his efforts, as long as they were gained through honest hard work and passion. If what they shared was a passion for their work, even though their paths ran in different directions, so be it.

Speaking of Adam, Alex glanced over to the passenger side of the car. Adam had just emerged and was leaning against the door, awkwardly grabbing his elbow. He looked uncomfortable and unsure of himself.

It had been an uphill battle to convince Adam to come today, to sit with him and Mike to discuss leadership qualities for an afternoon. Alex had done a lot of explaining and given Adam reassurance after reassurance that there were no strings attached to this visit. He just wanted Adam to listen to Mike and hear for himself what had influenced his father's efforts to improve their relationship. Besides, Alex thought, Mike's lessons were incredibly useful for anyone seeking direction in their lives. Adam could benefit greatly from his stories and the tenets that upheld his leadership system.

Alex walked over to Adam and put a hand on his shoulder. "Hey, thanks for coming today, buddy. I really appreciate it."

Adam shrugged. "I still don't totally get it, Dad. But..." he hesitated. "It seems like this Mike guy is important to you. And you've been way less annoying since you met him." He shot a wry half-smile at Alex.

Alex looked up at the sky, then back down at his son, smiling. "I'll take it, I guess." He squeezed Adam's shoulder and headed for the front door, Adam trailing behind.

Trust

Before they could reach it, the door swung open and Mike appeared in the doorway. "Welcome!" he boomed. He stepped forward and shook Alex's hand. "Alex, always a pleasure," he beamed.

"Likewise!" Alex responded, and he pulled Mike in for a hug. He stepped back and turned, waving Adam forward. "Mike Davis, I'd like you to meet my oldest son, Adam. Adam, this is Mike."

Adam walked up and extended his hand. "Hello, sir. It's a pleasure to meet you. Thank you for inviting me."

Mike laughed and embraced Adam's hand warmly in both of his. "Adam, the pleasure is all mine. I've heard so many wonderful things about you. When I heard your father was bringing a special guest this week, I hoped it might be you! I hope we can get to know each other a little better today."

Adam nodded in agreement. "I hope so too, sir." From the embrace and welcoming hug that Mike gave Adam, he could tell that this man was absolutely authentic and trustworthy. Adam had never felt so comfortable around a stranger. "There is some aura of selfless warmth about this guy," Adam thought.

"Oh, there's no need to call me sir" Mike waved his hand. "Please call me Mike." He smiled at Adam, then turned back toward the house. "Let's head back to the patio. We've got a lot to discuss today!"

***

"Now," Mike addressed Alex and Adam, after they had settled into their seats on the back patio. "Adam, you're probably wondering who I am and what your father is doing here every month."

"I've heard a little bit," Adam replied, somewhat hesitantly. "He told me something about a leadership system, and authenticity, and I've heard him chanting 'I can do' over and over again before important meetings. That's new, so I figured it had something to do with you."

Alex and Mike burst out laughing. "I had no idea you heard that!" Alex said, feeling a hot blush run up his neck. He rubbed his cheek in embarrassment. Adam grinned and nodded.

"Well, at least you're practicing!" Mike said. "And I'm glad to hear it." He turned to address Adam. "What your father is doing is practicing his *can-do* attitude and putting himself in a positive frame of mind. With optimism, anything is possible rather than *im*possible. Optimism is one of the core qualities of a new leadership method I'm developing: the COVETed leadership style."

"COVETed?" Adam asked. "You mean, like a leader that people want to follow?"

"Yes!" Mike encouraged. "That's part of it. The word 'COVET' comes from a Latin word Cupiditas meaning intense or passionate desire. It is also an acronym that stands for Courage, Optimism, Vision, Excellence, and – the one we'll be discussing today – Trust. A COVETed leader is one who practices all of these on a regular basis and makes a positive impact by making people feel bigger and better than who they think they are."

"The goal," Alex interjected, "as I see it, is to inspire people to feel and become their best selves. But you can't do that by learning only the basic skills of a leader. It requires leading with your whole mind, heart, and soul."

"Exactly," Mike replied. "As such, you can't simply apply this model to your workplace and your relationship with your coworkers. It's a lifestyle, an attitude. Do it consistently, and it improves communications and leadership in all areas of your life – professional, personal, familial, and sublimate. In short, Lead means to **L**et **E**very **A**ction of yours **D**efine you."

"Which is probably why I'm here," said Adam. He turned to his father, a small frown on his face. "Do you want to use this model to convince me to come work for you?"

"No!" exclaimed Alex. "Adam, that certainly wasn't the point of me bringing you here." He reached across the small table and grabbed Adam's arm. "I brought you here because, first, I wanted you to meet Mike, and second, I wanted you to understand that I'm learning how to approach our relationship differently. I know we've struggled to communicate lately, and we don't see eye to eye about your future."

"That's an understatement," Adam grumbled.

Alex sighed. "I suppose I deserve that. I haven't taken the time to really listen to you, and I haven't been fair about your desire to pursue your interests and hobbies. But Mike's lessons and stories have really shown me how to open up myself to others, and hear their needs and wishes in return. I want you to see for yourself how powerful these teachings are, and how much they've affected me in *all* areas of my life. Not just at work."

Adam hesitated, then nodded slowly. "Okay. And let me guess, there's probably something I can learn from them, too?"

Alex smiled. "If you want. I'm not here to push you, Adam. I only ask that you listen with an open mind. Mike has been so generous to share his time, his home, and his expertise with us. The least we can do is hear him out."

Mike, who had been watching the exchange with interest, coughed to break up a building tension between the two. "Well, as I said at the beginning, I'm not Santa Claus. I'm getting something out of this, too!"

He turned to Adam. "Your father has been a guinea pig of sorts for me, Adam. I wanted to test my concept in real time with an executive at Alex's level. I needed someone who was clearly a leader and runs a smaller business, but struggles with some of the core qualities we often take for granted in our leaders, like courage, authenticity, trust, to name a few." He slapped Alex on the back. "He's been a great partner these past few months. Willing to learn, but he's stubborn as all heck sometimes!"

Adam gave Mike a small half-smile. "Yeah, he does that at home, too. You should see him try to work the sound bar on our TV. He tries the same thing every time, and it never works!"

"Hey!" exclaimed Alex. "What is this, rib on Alex day?" They all laughed.

Mike pulled out his notebook and tossed it to Adam, who grabbed it and looked confused.

"Go on. Check it out." Mike waved at the book.

Adam looked down at the book, slowly opened it, and began riffling through the pages.

"This is the whole system. All my notes, research, thoughts, quotes, bits of my conversations with Alex and others. It's all here. The idea is to take this work and translate it into a practical course for anybody who wants to be a leader. It's my belief that there is a leader in each one of us that can be found at critical crossroads in our lives."

Adam nodded as he looked through the notebook. Alex stood up and pulled his chair closer to his son, peering over his shoulder as he read. "There's a lot in here about authenticity," Adam said. "And you've talked about it a few times today. Why isn't that one of your core qualities?"

"Excellent question!" Mike said. He rubbed his chin as he watched Adam skim slowly through the book. "Your dad asked the same thing when we started talking. Alex, do you want to take this one?"

"Sure," Alex said. "I remember you told me the story about Captain Swenson and his courage in battle to show his true self." Alex looked at Adam. "This Army captain ran into live fire to save his men who were under attack in Afghanistan. Again and again, he ran in to save whoever he could as quickly as possible. But an EMT with a GoPro attached to his helmet caught footage of him kissing one of his soldiers on the forehead before leaving to rescue others. It was a moment of incredible tenderness and caring." Alex hesitated, then continued.

"It was a heroic act. No one was watching him, and he didn't care, or wouldn't have cared if they were. He didn't know there was a camera recording it. He acted based on who he was as a man, as a leader. His, well, his tenderness required courage, optimism for success, the vision to plan the rescue operation, excellence in executing it, and an incredible amount of trust: C-O-V-E-T. But none of that would have been possible unless Captain Swenson knew himself, so deeply and so well, that he acted without hesitation and with a sense of the full responsibility of the love and empathy he felt for his soldiers. That kiss was a moment representing all of his courage, optimism, vision, excellence, and trust, all rolled into one."

"So ... authenticity is kinda like the basis for leadership?" Adam looked from his father to Mike and back to his dad.

"Yes!" both Mike and Alex replied, nearly in unison. Adam grinned and nodded his head.

Trust

"Okay, I can kinda see how that works," Adam said. "But what about being genuine? Is that the same thing as authentic?" He leaned towards Mike as the older man began to respond.

"Yes," Mike said, "but you don't always have to have a story to tell people to get them to believe in you like Captain Swenson, but you can always make people realize that they can have a story of their own."

Alex was relieved to see his son starting to relax. Adam asking Mike questions was a great start to the day. But then, Mike just seemed to have that effect on people. He recalled his first conversation with Mike in the diner, many months ago. Alex had shared some very personal things with him that day, and Mike had responded in kind. Yet he never felt pressured into sharing, and he never thought Mike would betray his confidence. He was sure Mike would uphold the same standards with his son.

"See, trust is key in knowing yourself and expressing true authenticity," Mike was saying as Alex turned back into the conversation. "If you can't trust yourself, first and foremost, you can't trust others. You can't be fully authentic with *anyone*. Trust is your internal compass. It's what defines you. It's a statement of what you stand for and what is really important to you. It has to be grounded in something bigger, something that shows your character. If the character is shaky and inconsistent then the whole system falls apart."

"Trust is our topic for the day, right?" Alex inquired.

"It sure is!" Mike replied. "We'll get into that in a second. But first, let's go for a walk. The leaves have started changing color, and I've got some amazing oak and sourwood trees on my property. I hope you like red and golden leaves. They're gorgeous. Let's go!"

***

The three men ambled through the trees behind Mike's house, the leaves crunching under their feet. Mike had neglected to tell them that his trees actually comprised a whole forest. Alex could only see thick foliage and huge trees surrounding the trails they followed. They walked mostly in silence, with Mike pointing out some interesting tree specimens and a hawk or two on occasion. After a particularly long stretch of companionable quiet, Mike spoke.

"Alex, how would you define trust?" he asked.

"Hmm," Alex thought for a moment, dodging a few stray branches that obscured the path. "I would say it's believing that others won't take advantage of your vulnerability. Before you can be vulnerable you have to have some amount of trust. It's being able to share deeply with others. It's a connection that can be very strong, yet very fragile. One breach of trust, and the thread is never the same again."

"That's great!" Mike agreed. "Adam, anything to add?"

"I guess it's also kind of about responsibility," Adam added. "If someone trusts me, I have to commit to that trust and keep it safe." He kicked a loose pebble down the path in front of them.

"Both wonderful answers! I'm going to add those to my notebook." Mike jotted down a few notes as they walked. "Your definitions get at the heart of why trust is so important but often so misunderstood. For one thing, it doesn't simply happen. Alex, as you point out, trust has to be *established,* and in most cases, earned. To do that, you have to be vulnerable with others and *empathize with them.*

"Maya Angelou once said, 'I've learned that people will forget what you said, people will forget what you did, but people will never forget how you made them feel.' Trust is about revealing your true self to others and enabling others to do the same with you. You're right, Adam. There is a great deal of responsibility there." Mike nodded at Adam.

"What about you?" Adam said. "How do you define trust?"

"Me?" Mike was silent for a few seconds, listening to the leaves crunch underfoot and the breeze in the trees.

"Trust, to me, is the ability to make others see the 'love behind the anger,' the 'sorrow behind the smile,' and the 'reason behind the silence.'"

"What do you mean? I don't get it," Adam said.

Trust

Mike stopped walking and turned to face the younger man. "When you get into an argument with your dad or your mom, do you feel like the only emotion they have towards you is anger, or resentment, or disappointment?"

The three men stopped as they came to a fire pit surrounded by benches.

"Have a seat," Mike said. Adam and Alex each took a seat.

"Well," Adam squirmed, reaching down to pick up a stick and twist it in his hands. "I do know that they often say things to me because they care. Even if I don't agree with their decisions."

"And how do you know that?" Mike asked.

Adam looked confused. "How do I know that they care?"

"Yes. Is it because they say it? Do they show it? If so, how do they show it?"

Adam glanced at Alex. "My dad does tell me he loves me," Adam sighed. "And he is always trying to get me to improve myself. I guess if he didn't care about me, he wouldn't care about those things." Adam looked down at the stick, breaking it in half before tossing it into the fire pit.

Alex nodded. "It's exactly because of that, son. I also know you can handle it," he said gently. "I don't want you to have any regrets later on in life, about your career and your aspirations. There are things that have caused me great pain, and today, I think I would have done certain things differently in my life. I want to spare you from those feelings."

Alex could see the realization creeping into his son's eyes. Adam brushed his hands off on his pants before responding. "I get that things happen, Dad. And I don't make it easy sometimes. But I just—" he sighed in frustration and ran his fingers through his hair.

"I just wish you could see *my* pain and frustration when you shoot down my ideas or don't really listen to my interests. There are things I want to do with my life that won't involve you. You have to trust that I'm capable of making my own decisions."

Alex nodded. "You're right," he said. "I'm causing the pain instead of seeing it. I'm starting to understand." He fell silent.

Mike cleared his throat and looked at both men. "That's the foundation of trust right there," he said softly. "You're actively building it." He pointed at

Adam. "It's the sorrow, pain and frustrations behind the smile." He then turned and pointed at Alex. "And the love behind the anger." Alex dipped his head in agreement, and Adam stared at the ground, nudging a root with his foot.

"Human beings are complex creatures," Mike said. "Often, our behavior masks deeper emotions. Sometimes we're too frightened or confused to reveal our emotions to others. Few men are raised to even acknowledge they have feelings. As the third part of the definition describes trust ... the reason behind the silence.

"The thing is we don't trust people to care about us as much as we care about them. Perhaps, in some cases, rightly so. But too often, we let negative emotions take over and cause more destruction than they have to. Anger, silence, and frustration, when wielded dishonestly, beget pain. So how do we stop the cycle?"

"I think what you're saying is we have to trust others. We have to take that initiative," Alex said.

"That is part of it. But it's not the full story."

"Ha!" groaned Alex. "I take it you're about to tell us another story."

"You know me too well, Alex!" Mike laughed. He turned to Adam. "I find stories a compelling way to illustrate my ideas. I can give you definitions and qualities until I'm blue in the face, but they don't really come alive until you hear how actual human beings actualize them in real situations."

Adam nodded. "Makes sense. So what's this story about?"

"About three years ago, I traveled to Sao Paulo with a group of leaders from around the world. These people came from all walks of life: foreign dignitaries, U.S. Senators, indigenous leaders, executives, professors, world-class athletes. The list goes on.

While there, I met a man named Paje Benki. He was a leader of the Ashaninka Nation, known throughout South America for their dignity, their spirit, and their resistance. When he was just ten years old, he became the 'paje' of his community, 'paje' being an honorary term bestowed upon the most important person in their community. Now, in the Ashaninka tradition, this is the person who contains within him all the knowledge and wisdom

Trust

of centuries and centuries of life. But it's not just about his people. It's also knowledge of everything that his people's survival depends on: the trees, the birds, the water, the soil, and the forest."

"Like a Shaman?" Adam asked.

"Well, like a Shaman and a historian, and a pastor and the wise man. He was the spokesman for his tribe and its traditions on all levels."

"Got it," Adam said.

Mike picked up a bright red leaf from the ground and studied it. He smiled and passed it silently to Adam before continuing.

"Though he was only ten, Paje Benki had learned from his grandfather before him that the biggest threat to his community was illegal logging. Outsiders would come into the beautiful forests of his homeland and cut down ancient mahogany trees, floating them down the river to world markets. So he went to his people and educated them on deforestation and how to protect and nurture their way of life. What he found was a lot of confusion and frustration among his people as to why these outsiders were coming to take their precious resources."

"That's totally understandable," Adam interrupted. "I mean, if I lived in the country or something and depended on the land for my livelihood or whatever, I'd be pissed if some people just came and started taking it away from me."

"True. You'd be pissed, but would you have the skills to reason with these people, or perhaps come to a mutual understanding on how you can both benefit from the land?" Mike asked. "These people did not, so they were taken advantage of. Once he turned eighteen, Benki realized he would have to seek help from the outside world in order to solve his plight.

"His people were naturally frightened for him and angry that he was abandoning them in their time of need. Benki tried to reassure them that he was leaving to find answers, but his people still didn't understand. No one had ever done that, or needed to. Nevertheless, Benki knew he had to go. So he left."

"Where did he go?" Alex asked.

"He traveled over 3,000 miles to Rio, to address attendees at the Earth Summit. He told them all about what was happening to his people and his land. He hoped people would listen, and he hoped they would provide him with ideas. Some did. Others did not.

"Regardless, he came back to his village full of ideas. Since that summit many years ago, Benki has built schools in his community to teach children to care for the forest. Together with other groups in the Amazon, he's led the reforestation of over twenty-five percent of the land that had been destroyed by the loggers. And he's brought the internet and satellite technology to the forest, which enables his people to monitor deforestation as well as communicate their successes and struggles to the rest of the world."

"I bet his people were happy about that," Alex said, looking at Adam. Adam nodded in agreement.

"They were happy to have their land partially restored," Mike acceded, "and they were eternally grateful for Benki's dedication to them and to their traditions. But they had to learn how to trust Benki over time, not just because of that one thing."

"People are never happy," Alex said. "You're only as good as the next great thing you do for them, never what you did."

"Optimism, Alex," Mike chided. "Optimism."

Alex blushed as Adam laughed.

"Got it. Go on."

Mike stood up and began piling dead leaves and twigs into the fire pit. "It's getting a bit chilly. How about a fire?"

Adam and Alex nodded. "Sure."

"Give me a hand, Adam," Mike said. Adam stood up and began collecting twigs. Alex walked behind a bench to a small woodpile and began pulling out larger sticks and logs. He laid them beside the pit, watching as his son quickly laid a fire in the pit. Alex looked surprised.

"Scouting, Dad," Adam said. "Told you I know more than you think I know."

Mike watched as Adam built up the fire, then handed him a lighter. Once the flames were licking the wood and the smell of wood smoke began to fill the air, he sat back down and motioned for Adam to do so as well.

Trust

"Many at the Earth Summit asked him, 'Why are you putting yourself at risk by traveling here? Aren't you afraid of the loggers and what they will do to your land and your people? How will you, one person from a small village, take them on?' What do you suppose was his answer? Why was he taking that risk?"

Adam shrugged, poking at the fire with a long stick. "That's a good question. I guess I would say he felt like he owed it to his people."

"In what way?" Mike urged. "You're on to it."

"Well," Adam said, "they trusted him to lead them, right? He left to find a solution to their problems and be a better leader. So, even if they didn't totally understand why he was getting the outside world involved, from his view he was doing it for them, even if they didn't totally trust he'd be able to find answers."

"Great explanation!" Mike cheered. Alex beamed. "What he did then was *honor their trust in him*. And that's how we stop the endless cycle of frustration and anger that can often occur in deep communication." He turned to Alex. "It's not just that we learn to trust others. We have to reciprocate that trust and, as leaders, take it even further.

"We have to do what is right and give it our all. Benki's story is one of endurance, total conviction and absolute faith that he had to honor his commitments to his people. He had the ability to keep the long-term sustainability of his tribe at the fore, and the willingness to endure insane hardship and obstacles to honor his commitments to his people beyond the mood. You cannot take your commitments lightly and honor them only when you are in a mood to do so and ignore when it doesn't suit you."

"I see," Alex nodded. "Leaders have to take the initiative to honor trust, especially in those cases of broken trust or tragedy." He stole a glance at Adam, who was focused intently on keeping the fire burning.

Alex could see now that he should have been the one to honor Adam's trust in him. He should have listened to his son, given him the benefit of the doubt and a chance to try it his way before bulldozing in with his own ideas. He shook his head.

Mike noticed Alex visibly struggling with his thoughts. "What's on your mind, Alex?" he asked quietly.

Alex sighed, then turned to his son. "Adam. I ... I owe you an apology. I realize now that not listening to you, pushing my own agenda, trying to get you to work for me – all of that was a lack of trust in you, and partly in myself. I was so concerned about your future that I thought I could create it. I didn't trust you to build it for yourself."

Adam smiled. He threw his stick into the fire. "Thanks, Dad. I really appreciate the apology. And I probably could have listened more, too," he admitted begrudgingly. "This trust stuff is making me realize that we haven't really talked to each other in awhile, you know?" He picked up the red leaf he'd set beside himself and handed it to his dad.

Alex smiled. "I think you're right. But hey, we're starting now, aren't we?" He leaned over and gently punched his son in his upper arm.

Adam stood up and wrapped his arms around his father in a big hug. Alex could tell Adam felt embarrassed about doing this in front of Mike, but he responded in kind, hugging back. Alex pulled back and put his hands on Adam's shoulders.

"I'm proud of you, son," he said quietly, willing himself not to cry as he was overcome with a strange feeling of vulnerability he hadn't experienced before.

Adam rolled his eyes. "Ok, thanks, Dad. I ... I'm proud of you, too," he blurted out. Then he shrugged out of Alex's grip. "But this doesn't mean I want to work for the company, okay? I want to figure things out on my own," he cautioned his father.

Alex nodded, a bright smile on his face. "Got it. Maybe we'll revisit in a few years. Never mind!" he said hastily, seeing the strong look of warning on Adam's face.

Mike chuckled and clapped a hand to each man's shoulder. "That's the spirit! Trust is everything. You've shown how a little openness and authenticity can help you build that trust that will serve you well as a leader."

The three men sat around the fire for another hour, talking and listening to Mike's stories and laughing. Adam tried to explain code to both men. The sun was beginning to drop in the sky, and the chill in the air became dampness and dusk.

"I hate to say it, but let's leave this great fire and head back to the patio and into the sun. Adam, there's a water barrel behind your bench. Go ahead and douse the fire."

Alex and Mike helped Adam pour several gallons of water from the barrel onto the fire, making sure it was out before heading down the path back to Mike's house.

***

"So," Mike said once they were settled on the patio again, this time with hot tea and light sandwiches before them. "Did you enjoy the Paje Benki story?"

Adam and Alex nodded. Alex swallowed a bit of sandwich before speaking. "Very much so! I especially liked his confidence, and his dedication to his people. It reminded me of the Wangari Matthai story."

"Absolutely!" Mike said. "Both worked hard to serve their people to the fullest extent possible in their capacities as leaders. What you've identified in these stories is the first of five tenets of trust under my COVETed leader system. Both Wangari and Benki honored their commitments, no matter how difficult the circumstances got."

"My teacher told us a quote that kinda reminds me of this," Adam said, reaching for another sandwich. "I think it went, 'A leader is someone who knows the way, goes the way, and shows the way.'"

"John C. Maxwell! Yes, that's a great bit of advice, and very apropos," Mike said. "It's all about how you follow through. Broken promises create problems, so you have to go beyond the mood. You might break your promises if you don't commit one hundred percent. COVETed leadership has a lot to do with your integrity as a leader."

Alex nodded vigorously. "That's what I'm seeing with my coworkers. When I tell them I'm going to do something and I follow through with it, the resulting communications or project or whatever is *so* much stronger. Being negative causes us to spiral downward. I didn't see that so much before, but I do now. I think we forget the power of integrity, action, and positivity to produce exponentially more for the effort."

"Great point," Mike said. "I have to warn you that it is not that you will never have to break a promise. We have to be realistic. Sometimes circumstances beyond your control prevent you from being able to keep a promise. It's having the integrity to go back to the person you made the promise to and own up to not being able to keep that promise. You need to honestly apologize and promise to make it up before the person starts to guess the reasons or wonder what happens next. Integrity means being honest and having strong moral principles such that your thoughts, words, and action are in absolute sync, and you are willing to give it all.

"And, I think this leads very well into another tenet of trust: connecting at a deeper level. Keeping promises is not about upholding your word, come what may, or about absolute perfection. It's about establishing a deep connection. Really, that's at the heart of what you're doing with your coworkers. That is the key to trust – connecting at such a deep level that people around you can see the love behind the anger and the reason behind the silence. They see that you are doing your absolute best to make things happen for them. They see that, and not so much the broken promise. That doesn't mean you don't have to fight to keep every promise. It means in the very rare times you can't, your people will understand."

"Yes, and what we did today" Alex agreed, turning to Adam, who nodded between bites of his sandwich. Alex and Mike chuckled at the sight.

"Yes, absolutely," Mike said. "I'm reminded of the story of the blind CEO. Have you heard this one, Alex?"

Alex shook his head. "It doesn't sound familiar."

"Well, remember my example of the actor, Isaac, who was born with sight but saw his vision deteriorate in his teens? This is a similar story, except Srikanth Bolla was born completely blind to a poor family in India. He was often shuffled to the back of the classroom and routinely had difficulty finding audio versions of his textbooks. But he never let that keep him down. He graduated from MIT when he was eighteen years old and started a company that employs disabled, uneducated people to manufacture eco-friendly and disposable consumer packaging solutions. Right now, he has four production plants in operation with a fifth on the way next year."

"Wow," said Adam, listening intently. "And he runs the whole company? That must be so hard!"

"You and I would think so!" Mike chuckled. "But Srikanth's mantra is simple: I don't need to see them as long as I *connect* to them at a deeper level. What matters to him are the deep relationships he builds with his workers and those he serves. He does this by demonstrating empathy, leading by example, but also by being humble. He is very proficient at what he does and has mastered the tricks of his trade through dedication, hard work, and absolute diligence.

"Yet, he's not afraid to ask for help if he needs it, without being afraid or unapologetic about appearing weak, whether the help he needs is related to his disability or not. The key is that he is willing to admit that he does not know it all and that the reservoir of knowledge is so deep and wide that it is not possible for someone to have an understanding of everything about everything.

"Leadership is full of paradoxes. While as a leader, you are required to be convincing and show the desired direction, it's not your job to be right all the time. And once you are clear about this paradox, you'll have no problem seeking help and saying 'I don't know, and I need help.'"

"I see," Alex said. He chewed slowly and took a sip of tea before speaking. "So this relates back to courage, too?"

"Courage, but it seems like he'd have to be pretty connected to himself to do all of that," Adam said. "You know, how we were talking about authenticity earlier? He'd have to be a pretty genuine guy."

Mike laughed and slapped the table. "By jove, Watson, I think he's got it!" He pointed at Adam. "You've just identified a very important tenet of trust. Identifying your inner core — being really in touch with oneself, being your true self. As Srikant says, 'I don't mind being vulnerable. I don't waste time feeling bad for myself.'

"I am okay with what I cannot do being blind because there is so much that I can do. You are who you are – the unadulterated, unpretentious and unashamedly you, which is fundamentally critical for establishing trust in and with others. You have to be true to yourself for your word to mean anything at all. You can't be flip-flopping back and forth. And, yes," Mike turned to Alex, "this involves a great deal of courage, too. And vulnerability."

"Vulnerability?" asked Adam. "What does this have to do with that? Isn't vulnerability about showing weakness?"

"Not at all," replied Mike. "But that's a common misconception. Vulnerability is what allows us to connect with others without the defensive walls we so often construct to make ourselves seem bigger, better, faster, stronger, smarter. Those barriers often *prevent* us from seeing other people as they are. They're a façade; they're not real. But they're certainly easier for most people to handle."

"They seem that way, at first," Alex admitted. "But they cause so many problems down the line. If you're committed for a long time, though, I can see how it would be hard to drop those walls."

"Absolutely," said Mike. "Breaking free of those defensive routines requires a willingness to embrace vulnerability. Often, that willingness only surfaces at major crossroads in life. If that's what it takes, then so be it. But I try to encourage a more proactive approach to embracing vulnerability and being your most authentic self.

"I should also point out that *this* kind of vulnerability is different than personal vulnerability. The vulnerability we feel when faced with something we can't handle, like brain surgery or a devastating natural disaster, is a human condition totally unrelated to leadership. The kind of vulnerability I'm referencing here has to do with the state of being exposed to the possibility of attack, harm, or criticism – all things a leader will face at some point in his or her life. The vulnerability a leader needs to have includes confidence in their own abilities and skills so they *can* listen to feedback from those around them. To be a vulnerable leader, you have to avoid approval addiction and tame your ego."

Mike turned to Adam. "Does that make sense? We could spend all afternoon talking about vulnerability! It's a complex subject. But being vulnerable is being authentic, which is a profound way of connecting deeply with others, sharing yourself with those who care about you."

Adam nodded. "It makes sense, and I'm glad you clarified the difference. But how do you get leaders to take the more proactive approach?"

"Great question," replied Mike. "When you truly believe in your authenticity, then your sense of self-worth and confidence will help you overcome approval addiction."

"Approval addiction? That's an interesting phrase," Adam said.

"Any addiction is toxic, young man," Mike joked. "But the moment you get desperately obsessed with seeking approval of others, you are likely to lose your authentic self. Your true self is not something you go looking for in others. You be who you are because then you are not wasting energy and time hiding your faults and trying to show only the side that will get you others' acceptance.

"You must be absolutely willing to pay the price of not being liked or rejected by some. You proactively and intentionally choose to live a life that is meaningful to you, and that actually brings out the most likeable part of you. You appear more genuine to others, and that will breed a sense of intimacy, transparency, and honesty. People will instantly know that you are not manipulative or deceptive, and will perceive you as authentic because there will be clarity and purity in what you say. Your words and deeds will be in harmony because they represent your core values and morals."

"I have a question," Adam quipped. "If you try to be your authentic self regardless of trying to be liked by others, or you try not be afraid of losing some friends, doesn't that make you egotistical?"

"Brilliant question, Adam," Mike said. Alex shuffled in his chair with pride.

"There is a thin line between *confidence* and *arrogance*. Failure to recognize that will leave you fractured inside," Mike said. "Your ego is the most volatile part of your personality. It swings between two extremes. Your ego could make you feel extremely cocky and all powerful, or it could make you feel extremely shriveled and disgraced. It is important to develop an ego that exudes confidence and commands respect from others. It gives others the aura of confidence in the leader and helps them overcome their insecurities. It fuels growth and breaks through the threshold of fear.

"It is necessary for a leader to have a well-developed ego because that's what keeps them on track. They need to have an uncompromising commitment to getting things done, and the confidence, commitment, and dedication to exceed expectations – all things that come from a healthy ego. But you also need to keep that ego in check. You need to learn to tame it. As they say, '*Seek the world, but don't get consumed by the idea that you are the world.*'

"One of my favorite quotes is by Baroness Campbell, 'Humility is not thinking less of yourself; it is thinking about yourself less.'

"This brings me to the last two tenets of trust," said Mike holding up two fingers. "Number one is you have to practice mindfulness."

"Mindfulness?" asked Adam. "What's that?"

"I think I can answer this one, Mike," Alex said. He turned to Adam.

"Mindfulness is about being present in the moment and focusing your energy on that. You have to learn how to be aware of your thoughts, emotions, and how your body's feeling in the present, and you have to accept whatever you're feeling without judgment."

"Don't get it," Adam frowned.

"Well, if you sit here and just notice your thoughts, without judging them, like, "Oh, I'm thinking about being anywhere but here, but Dad would be pissed, so that's bad," Alex joked.

"Dad!"

"But it's true," Alex continued. "Once you intentionally start looking at your thoughts and feelings, you'll notice they're all over the place. There's no order. It's like trying to herd squirrels by turning cats loose."

Mike laughed out loud at Alex's metaphor. "True," he said.

"Mindfulness just sort of forces you to contend with your true self and connect with your inner core and thoughts – although not usually the first time you do it. It takes practice," Alex said. "Lots of practice."

"Well said, Alex," Mike said. "It's talked about a lot in meditation circles, but mindfulness is a useful way to keep the distractions and walls at bay. Once you practice it enough, you find that your presence is a gift to others."

"Do you have to meditate, or sit, or pray, or something?" Adam asked.

"No, no … it's something you do as you're going through your day. You start off learning to be mindful by practicing in a room, maybe your bedroom or the back yard. Just find someplace quiet and sit. Close your eyes and pay attention to your thoughts. When you're going about your day and something angers you, stop and look at your anger. How does it feel?

"Where is it in your body? What color is it? The idea is to become aware of it without being triggered by it. Again, takes practice. But you'll notice how you react to things if you do it consistently – usually in about a week or so," Mike said. He turned towards Alex and said, "Remember Viktor Frankl? He said, 'Between stimulus and response, there is a space. In that space is our power to choose our response. In our response lies our growth and our freedom.'"

"Of course, I do. I think it took me a month to come to grips with that thought," Alex admitted, blushing. "I'm slow."

Mike laughed. "I'm not even going to tell you how long it took me, months maybe." He paused to think back to his first experience. "I don't remember, but it was a while. Still, I encourage you both to practice being mindful. And be generous with your small acts of presence and thoughtfulness. Alex, it sounds like you've been practicing this with your coworkers quite a bit!"

"I have, though I don't think I realized it!" laughed Alex. "I've found that taking the time to chat about their ideas, listen to their struggles, and just be with them in those moments has worked wonders on productivity and overall confidence within the company. We've launched a ton of new projects and people just seem…" Alex shrugged. "I don't know. Happier. There's a lightness and joy in the office that I don't recall seeing before."

"It's funny that that sounds foreign to you, Alex, because that's the way it should be! It's not the exception to have dreary, uninspired working spaces, but we've defaulted to that for some reason. But no worries, Alex. Always remember that 'Today is the first day of the rest of your life,' so whenever you realize it, it marks the beginning. You've begun to build towards something much better, and trust is at the foundation of that growth.

"Which leads me to my fifth tenet of trust: believe, yet authenticate."

"Huh?" Adam said. Alex looked confused, too. "Are you saying don't be too trusting?"

"I'm saying everything has to have balance," Mike replied gently. "Trust is fragile, as I believe you mentioned earlier." He gestured toward Alex. "You should trust people, but be aware of the human tendency towards exploitation and manipulation. Most people won't do it with malicious intent. It's perhaps what they're used to. It's part of their subconscious. Just be aware of your own strengths. Be confident and be present in your interactions. If you do this, the rest will take care of itself. "The Russian, 'Doveryai, no proveryai.' It means trust, but verify."

"I am confused," said Alex.

Mike looked deep into Alex's eyes and said, "Trust is a very natural human instinct, but it is also very contextual. You don't want to be in a situation that you believe every word you hear from everybody. You need to build trust over a period of time. When you first met me, I bet you were skeptical of me and my philosophy, but trust has built over the last few months. One big reason for that was that I was holding you accountable for practicing what you were learning, and you were being competent in upholding the pillars of the COVETed leader model, so it became sort of a covenant."

"Oh. Oh! Now I get it," Alex said. He slapped his hand down on the table twice. "I get it."

"I have a 2%-98% trust model. This is 'Find the 2% in anyone and stretch it to the optimum comfort level. Then, avoid the 2% in everyone to stay clear of the *back-room*," said Mike.

Alex had a very perplexed look on his face and so did Adam. "I don't get it," Adam said. He frowned.

"I'll explain. I believe that as human beings we all have 2% in common, so no matter who we meet, we have a 2% connection and trust in each other. No matter who you are, that tiny connection is a given percentage. This could be

Trust

in the form of a simple 'Hello' or just a nod of approval or a smile at a stranger. But once you start to know the other human and establish a connection, this trust percentage starts to increase.

"With each person, this percentage gets settled at a certain level depending on how much we would like to trust each other. The normal range of trust people establish is anywhere between 50% to 70% – with colleagues, friends and peers. It is with only a select few that this percentage goes beyond 70%. That 70% typically happens with our parents, our spouse and children, or our very close friends. However, no matter how close you get to any person, even your spouse, you must not cross the 98% mark."

"You mean the maximum trust we can establish is 98%?" Alex asked.

"Absolutely," said Mike. "There is a 2% part of every human that should be left absolutely private. No one, no matter what the relationship is, can get access to that 2%. Never tread on that 2%, or let anyone have access to your 2%. I call it the *back-room*."

"Hmm ... that's interesting," Alex said.

Adam jumped in and exclaimed, "Wow! That's so cool. You mean there is part of your life where you don't allow access to anyone, and that could be any percentage, starting from 2% on up?"

"Yup," said Mike.

"Don't get any wild ideas, my friend," said Alex as he looked at Adam's excitement.

"Well, that is what earning trust means, Alex. You don't put rules around that percentage. You have to earn it gradually. You're always trying to keep increasing that percentage, but that 2% is sacred," Mike said.

"I love that," Adam said. His excitement was evident. His face flushed red, and his breathing was fast. "But that applies to you too, young man," said Mike.

"Of course, I do understand that," Adam said. "But this is really deep."

Mike stood up and stretched. The sun was low on the horizon now, and the air had turned breezy and cold. The day was coming to a close.

"Well, I think this is a perfect place to end our little experiment, Alex, and also a perfect place to make a new beginning with Adam," Mike said. He reached out a hand to Alex.

"Alex, thank you so much for your generosity and willingness to play along with me these past several months. I've so enjoyed our time together, and I hope we can continue to connect. My door is always open to you."

Alex stood and shook his hand. "Likewise, Mike," he replied, a little choked up. "I'm so honored we could work on this together, and I'm incredibly grateful for the opportunity to learn from you and get to know you. It's been a pleasure through and through."

Mike smiled at Alex, then turned his attention to Adam. "Young man, thank you for coming along with your father today. I'm sure it seemed strange at first, but I do hope you found some benefit in listening to an old man's stories and life lessons for an afternoon."

"Absolutely," Adam reassured him. "I really wasn't sure what to expect, but I've learned a lot from you today. You and my dad," he said, glancing over at Alex.

Alex nodded. "Likewise, son."

"Well, that's life, right?" Mike noted. "If we're not constantly learning, then what's the point? Mark Twain has a famous quote about that. This one I've memorized.

"He said, 'Twenty years from now, you will be more disappointed by the things you didn't do than by the ones you did do. So throw off the bowlines, sail away from safe harbor, catch the trade winds in your sails. Explore. Dream. Discover.'"

"Well said," Alex said. Adam nodded.

Mike smiled. "I'll send you off with that then. Let me walk you to the door."

"Hey, Mike," Alex leaned in to the older man as they approached the front door. "You never told me the resolution of that one story."

"Which story?" asked Mike.

"You know, the one about the CEO and the driver. I've been waiting for months to hear the rest of that one!" Alex replied, laughing.

Trust

"Oh yeah! I completely forgot," Mike slapped his hand on his forehead. "Forgetful me. Let me tell you the conclusion here quickly."

"Dad, I'm going to head to the car," Adam called out from ahead.

Alex waved in acknowledgment and turned back to Mike. "Let's hear it!"

"So, as you may recall," Mike began, "I told you the story of a CEO I used to work for who defied every definition of a great leader. He was successful, yes, but incredibly rude, arrogant, and utterly uninterested in forging deep connections with any of his employees. After a mix-up in schedules, his company driver dropped him off at the wrong location."

"And you were tasked with firing him, right?" said Alex. "I remember. That sounded like such a tough conversation." He winced.

"It was," Mike agreed. "But the driver could not have been more supportive of *me*. I still remember how he stood up for me and my career when he was the wronged party. He truly exhibited all the qualities of a COVETed leader in this one selfless act.

"Anyway, the story continues. Many years later, the executive was traveling to India with his wife on vacation. One late evening while on vacation, his wife developed complications with her renal system. Both of her kidneys failed, and she was rushed to the hospital. She needed an immediate kidney transplant. There was no time to transport her back to the United States. The operation would have to happen in India."

"I bet her husband wasn't too happy about that," commented Alex.

"He was not," confirmed Mike. "In fact, he didn't believe they could do the transplant up to his specifications. The arrogance in this man! But in that situation, little else could be done. So the surgery was performed, and his wife received a kidney from an anonymous donor. She made an incredible recovery. The doctors and nurses at the hospital saved her life.

"Upon seeing her recovery, her husband had a complete change of heart. His wife's close brush with death made him see how cruel, uncaring, and arrogant he had been to those in his life.

"So he began to make amends. He started with those doctors and nurses who had saved his wife's life. When he got to the young doctor who was on duty the night his wife had been brought in and who this arrogant CEO had been pathetically rude to, he asked him one simple yet profound question. 'Who is the leader who taught you be so calm and composed?' he asked. 'He must be an incredible, talented, and passionate individual.'

"'He is,' replied the doctor. 'He's my father. You can meet him tomorrow morning. He comes every day to voluntarily attend to the patients in the hospital."

The next morning the CEO was anxiously waiting to meet this gentleman. In walked an old, frail person who had humility written all over him. It was very easy for the CEO to guess that this would be the person.

"This is my father," the doctor said. The CEO went over to the person and extended his hand to shake, and as soon as the doctor's father saw the CEO, he most politely and with utmost humility held his hand with both his hands and said, 'I am glad your wife is out of danger, sir." He then addressed the CEO by his name.

The CEO was surprised that the gentleman knew his name and said, "Oh, so you have done some homework on me!"

"No sir, I have known you for a long time."

The CEO was shocked but curious. The gentleman very politely said, 'Sir, I worked for you. I used to be your driver a long time ago.'"

Mike paused. Alex was hanging on his every word.

"Who was it?" Alex breathed in astonishment.

"Would you believe," Mike replied, "that it was his one time company driver?"

"No!" gasped Alex. "Are you serious? What are the odds?"

"It's remarkable, right? And, what's more, the kidney that his wife received came from the driver's wife."

"Oh, my God! This is unbelievable!" Alex all but shouted. He laughed. "That's an incredible story. That could be a movie!"

"Or a book," Mike responded, chuckling along with Alex.

"Or a book," Alex agreed. "But ... I'm not sure I get the point. It seems so remarkable that those connections would happen in the first place. What's the lesson here?"

"Remember, I told you that life is all about experiences and expressions that you go through as part of this huge cycle in the universe. Anybody who is where he or she is today is there by chance and could have been very easily in another place with different circumstances. So if you are lucky to be in a privileged place, you have no right to be mean and discourteous to any underprivileged fellow human.

"This is what COVETed leaders do. They make others feel bigger and better than who they think they are. Just because the CEO was in a position of power did not make him the COVETed leader. On the contrary, think about it," Mike said. "The driver and his wife clearly knew who would receive the kidney. That was not a coincidence. So they had a choice to make: donate a compatible kidney to someone in dire need, or deny or ignore the request as a reproach and revenge of sorts. They preferred prudence over power."

"This makes such a strong lesson. It's a powerful conclusion to what you started with – Courage," Alex admitted. "And it did change things, didn't it?"

"Absolutely! Deciding to donate a kidney is never an easy decision or process to undergo, but the choice itself was a simple act. And one act was all it took to change a man's life."

"And he, in turn, changed others' lives after that, I'm sure," said Alex.

Mike tipped his head in agreement. "Exactly."

"And that's the heart of this story. You can break the cycle at any time. All it takes is one decision, one act, one choice. Any of us at any time can choose to change the trajectory of things gone awry.

"All of the stories I've told you illuminate this. The beauty of the COVETed leadership model is that its pillars and tenets reward honest effort given *when the recipient is ready to give it*. That's what you had to learn with your business, and with your family. I think you've succeeded admirably in both regards, from what I've seen.

"Remember, I told you that the word 'COVET' is Cupiditas in Latin, meaning intense and passionate desire. Well, sometimes the intensity could go *awry* and become very detrimental to one's own being, as with the CEO when he was full of himself, an arrogant executive. So it is important to acknowledge the complexity while recognizing the beauty of being a leader."

Alex smiled and shook his head. "Well, I owe you for introducing me to this system in the first place. It's changed my life, too, although perhaps not as dramatically as the executive and his wife."

Mike laughed. "Don't be so sure! Over time, you too will see dramatic changes at work and in your relationships with your family, friends, and colleagues.

"In the meantime, I only ask that you pass along what you've learned here. It doesn't matter how you do it, but I firmly believe knowledge like this should be shared. So go forth!" Mike gestured to the door. "And good luck. Keep me updated on how things go. I'm always eager to hear your stories."

"Will do!" Alex hugged Mike for a final time and walked through the door. Before he reached his car, he turned back and looked at Mike. "It'll be nice to have some stories to share with you for a change!" Alex shouted.

Alex could still hear Mike laughing as they drove down the driveway and turned onto the street.

IN SUMMARY:

Trust is the ability to make others see the love behind the anger; sorrow behind the smile and the reason behind the smile.

The five tenets of trust are:

- **Identify your inner core.** Our inner core is who we are at our core. Our core is the foundation that our personality, work ethic, morals, and self is based on. Understanding our core means being true to oneself, letting go of all our fears and any emotional baggage or relationships that keep us from seeing who and what that core is. It's more than self-reflection.

It's self-study and the ability to honestly recognize, assess, and appraise oneself or define yourself.

It's being able to look into the mirror and face yourself, and develop a complete harmony in your thought, word, and action. It is avoiding pretense to get the approval of others or be liked by others. It's being willing to pay the price and lose those connections that cannot accept you as your true self. It's developing an ego that inspires others and compels them to follow and support you while ensuring that it can be tamed and managed.

- **Connect at a deeper level.** Many of our most important relationships, family and work specifically, are superficial. We fear losing or damaging those relationships if we offend or anger the other, so we keep our interactions shallow to avoid the things we think might cause friction. As a result, we fail to connect at a deeper level with those who matter most. By connecting at a deeper level, we learn to develop empathy, which helps us understand others better by walking as they say, "in someone else's moccasins."

  We collaborate and integrate to make the circle of influence bigger and stronger by avoiding any ambiguities, establishing more intimate and personal understanding and a more intentional and curious approach to engaging a process of greater good. Connecting at a deeper level means being willing to admit that you do not know all and can appeal to others' expertise while seeking help.

- **Believe, yet authenticate.** Trust does not just happen. It requires intentionality and is contextual. The 2%-98% trust model is based on basic human instinct that people are by and large trustworthy, but you need to gradually discover the extent of trust that you can sustain. This approach will help us overcome the insecurities we develop due to our social conditioning. We learn to think, examine, and then establish trust that will safeguard us from exploitation.

- **Honor commitments.** Success really comes from keeping your promises to yourself and others. Honoring your commitments, no matter how small, is the key to creating trust.

    Signs of a hypocrite have been described as "when he speaks he lies; when he makes promises he breaks them; and when he is trusted he betrays trust" as opposed to a person with integrity who does what he promises, builds an aura of consistency, and can be depended on to always do what is right. Avoid making snap, emotional commitments. But once you make a commitment, give it your best with total passion.
- **Be mindful.** Control of your life, emotions, actions, and reactions comes from being mindful of yourself and who you are in every moment. Being fully present helps you stay calm and centered.

    Being mindful is being aware that the only time that is real is *now*, and the future is an opportunity to maximize your potential and growth, appreciating the people around you and acknowledging them for who they are. And finally being mindful is being generous with small acts of kindness and compassion, and making others feel bigger and better than who they think they are, and effectively playing the role of a COVETed leader.

Chapter Nine

A FINAL WORD

If you found this book useful, please let me know by visiting my website at www.thecovetedleader.com. I welcome all your thoughts and suggestions.

Also, please consider putting up a review of this book on Amazon. The review doesn't have to be long. Even three sentences will do. Reviews matter greatly as they indicate to people that a book is worth reading. They truly make or break an author. So, if you did like what you read, please share it. Amazon is the best location to put up a review because more than 80% of all books are sold there.

Finally, thank you. I appreciate you. You made a difference in my life by reading this book. I sincerely hope that it made a difference in your life, too, and that you will spread the insights you got from this book and gift it by passing on your new wisdom—even this or another copy of this book—to someone you care about.

P.S. If you would like to get in touch with me, please feel free to email me at fazlsiddiqui@gmail.com or fazl@thecovetedleader.com.

Acknowledgements

Asked to write a page on acknowledgements by my publicist, I really struggled to get started as the list of people who I would like to thank is so long with each being a COVETed Leader in their own right. But I had to start somewhere so here is how I would begin…

First, I would like to express my deepest gratitude to my God who gave life, gave me the capability and the opportunity to write this book.

Life is a journey of episodes – some happy and some not so pleasant, but every time I went through an episode in my life, I fell in love with my wife even more, so I have fallen in love with my wife over and over during the last 25 years of our blissful marriage. Although almost 10 years my junior Zulaikha has always been way stronger, wiser and a great source of support every time we experienced a tough phase in our life. I have always been a dreamer and had it not been for her practical wisdom things would have been very different and difficult today. I would not be able to thank her enough for always being there for me and supporting me with all her heart.

I also want to thank my beautiful children Safaa who has always been the delight of my life and Bilaal who demonstrates a serene sense of rare-air stability and strength (that he gets from his grandfather), and the two latest additions to the family, my son-in-law Sufiyan and adorable grandson Faisal.

This list, as I said is going to be unending, but some notable people that deserve special mention are my parents and of course my eldest brother Anwar Khursheed who has been the *de facto* father in my life.

I would also like to thank my colleague Salma Al-Hajjaj with whom I have engaged in some very interesting intellectual discussions that helped me crystallize my thoughts. I would like to thank some other very dear genuine friends like Rana Al-Khalid, Aijaz Ahmed Sarfaraz and a few others who were always there to listen and support me, I have tremendous regard for these selfless people.

I cannot forget to thank some Kuwait Oil Sector leaders such as Nader Sultan, Ghazi Al-Mutairi, Hosnia Hashim and many more who made an effort to spend their valuable time sharing their thoughts and inspiring personal stories.

I would also like to express my gratitude for all those COVETed Leaders out there who are *making a great difference in the world by making theirs and the lives of those around them extraordinarily fulfilling* and also those readers who will get some inspiration from this book to do the same.

Finally, I would like to thank my publicist, Melissa G Wilson, and editor, Becky Blanton, for their untiring efforts in giving the book an interesting shape.

www.ingramcontent.com/pod-product-compliance
Lightning Source LLC
Chambersburg PA
CBHW070103120526
44588CB00034B/2017